MW01156676

Steck-Vaughn
School Supply

CORE
SKILLS

Science

GRADE
6

Contents

Introduction

Steck-Vaughn's *Core Skills Science* series offers parents and educators high-quality, curriculum-based products that align with the Common Core Standards for Reading in the Sciences for grades 1–6. The *Core Skills Science* books provide informative and grade-appropriate readings on a wide variety of topics in life, earth, and physical science. Two pages of worksheets follow each reading passage. The book includes:

- clear illustrations, making scientific concepts accessible to young learners

- engaging reading passages, covering a wide variety of topics in life, earth, and physical science

- logically sequenced activities, transitioning smoothly from basic comprehension to higher-order thinking skills

- comprehension questions, ascertaining that students understand what they have read

- vocabulary activities, challenging students to show their understanding of scientific terms

- critical thinking activities, increasing students' ability to analyze, synthesize, and evaluate scientific information

- questions in standardized-test format, helping prepare students for state exams

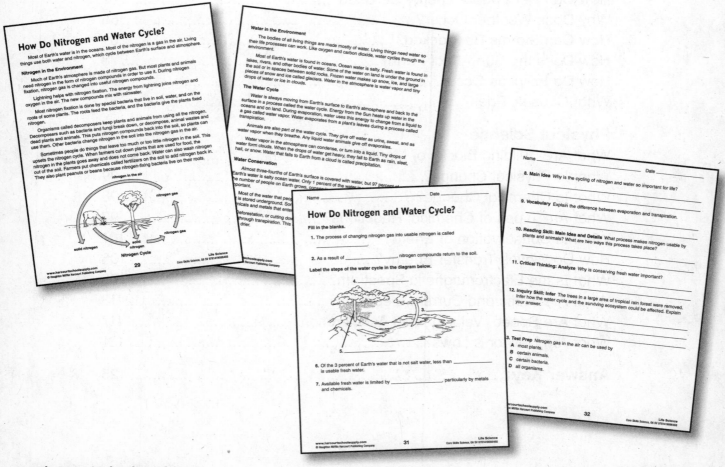

How Do Scientists Classify Organisms?

The Six Kingdoms

A species is a specific kind of living thing. Scientists use a system of biological classification to put millions of species into groups based on their characteristics. Then scientists worldwide can recognize those common names.

The largest group in this system is called a kingdom. Many scientists use six kingdoms. Bacteria have two kingdoms. Protists, fungi, plants, and animals each have one.

To group organisms, scientists study the internal and external structures of living things. They also study individual cells and the chemical processes inside cells. Scientists then use this information to group species according to how closely related they are.

Classifying Tools

One night you see a flying animal. Is it a bird? Then you see it has fur. Do birds have fur? No, so it cannot be a bird. You see that the wings look like skin stretched over bone.

What animal can fly, has fur, and has wings like skin? It must be a bat. The answer to each question helped you determine what the animal is. Each answer also helped you determine what the animal could not be.

To identify living things, scientists use a tool called a dichotomous key. "Dichotomous" means "divided into two parts," so the key gives two characteristics to choose between. Each choice leads to another pair of characteristics. Each choice narrows the possibilities of what the organism can be.

Bacteria

Bacteria are small organisms with a single cell that has no nucleus. This makes bacteria different from other living things. Bacteria must be seen with a microscope. There are more bacteria than any other organism, and they live almost everywhere on Earth.

Some kinds of bacteria are useful. Bacteria in your stomach help you digest food. Other types of bacteria are harmful and can cause disease, like strep throat.

Bacteria are separated into two kingdoms. Archaebacteria is one kingdom. These bacteria have lived on Earth longer than any other organism. Today they live under conditions that would kill other living things. Eubacteria cannot live in such harsh conditions. Most bacteria are eubacteria. Eubacteria get food in a variety of ways. They use the Sun's energy or eat nonliving and living materials.

Protists

A protist is an organism that may have some characteristics of fungi, plants, and animals. The organisms in Kingdom Protista are very different from one another. Most protists have just a single cell. Each protist cell has a nucleus. The cells of protists also have special structures that do certain things for the cell, such as changing food into energy.

Animal-like protists are called protozoa. Protozoa cannot make their own food, so they get their food from their surroundings. Most protozoa can move through their environment. Some seem to slip and slide like jelly. Others use moving tail-like structures or fine hairs. A paramecium, for example, is covered with hair-like structures that help it move.

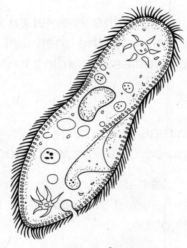

paramecium

Algae are plant-like protists. They use energy from the Sun to make their own food. Like plants, they make oxygen. Many organisms depend on them for food and oxygen.

Some protists have the characteristics of fungi. They get their food from their surroundings. Some reproduce through spores as fungi do. Many can move from place to place, but they move slowly. Fungus-like protists attack crops and also animals, such as fish.

Fungi

Organisms in Kingdom Fungi can be small, one-celled organisms, or they can grow to large masses as wide as 1 foot or more. Scientists have identified over 70,000 species of fungi.

Like all other kingdoms except bacteria, fungi cells have nuclei. Their cell walls are made of the same substance as the hard shells of insects.

Fungi do not make or eat food. Instead, fungi absorb nutrients from their environment. They decompose, or break down, the tissues of other organisms. Fungi cannot move from place to place. Yet they can grow very quickly over a surface. Their spores can travel very far in wind or water.

How Do Scientists Classify Organisms?

Write answers to the questions on the lines below.

1. Explain how scientists use a dichotomous key for classifying organisms.

_____

_____

_____

_____

2. Explain how bacteria can be useful.

_____

_____

_____

3. What is the most abundant organism on Earth?

_____

4. What are two characteristics of protozoa?

_____

5. What kind of organism can have some characteristics of fungi, plants, and animals?

_____

6. What kinds of bacteria have lived on Earth longer than any other organism?

_____

7. Main Idea What are two goals of the system used to classify organisms?

_____

_____

8. Vocabulary What is biological classification?

_____

_____

9. Reading Skill: Classify You are trying to identify a one-celled organism. You know that the organism has a cell nucleus and produces its own food from sunlight. What kingdom does the organism belong to?

_____

10. Critical Thinking: Evaluate Scientists once classified living things into only two kingdoms: plants and animals. Why do you think they use six kingdoms today?

_____

_____

11. Inquiry Skill: Compare What are two differences between organisms in Kingdom Protista and Kingdom Fungi?

_____

_____

_____

12. Test Prep The cells of organisms in the _____ kingdom do not have nuclei.

   A protist

   B plant

   C bacteria

   D fungi

How Are Plants Classified?

The Plant Kingdom

More than 300,000 species of plants live on Earth. Yet members of Kingdom Plantae share certain characteristics. Plants have many cells that have chloroplasts, the cell parts that make food. Plants have tissues and organs.

Plants need water to survive, but some plants can live in dry places. The way in which plants transport water, or carry it to all parts of the plant, is one characteristic that scientists use to put plants into groups. Scientists also classify plants based on how they reproduce.

Nonvascular plants absorb water, which slowly passes directly from cell to cell. Nonvascular plants do not have tissues to transport water, so they must live near a water source. The lack of a water transport system keeps nonvascular plants from growing very tall. Many barely reach a few inches tall when they are fully grown.

Vascular plants have tissues that act like tubes. This tissue takes up water and nutrients from the soil through the plant's roots. This means that vascular plants do not have to live close to a body of water. The vascular system provides support and allows plants to grow very tall. Over time, vascular plants have developed ways of living in most climates, dry and wet.

Ferns

The fern is a common type of vascular plant. It has roots, stems, and leaves that contain vascular tissue. Ferns do not have seeds, so they reproduce by making spores. A spore has half the beginning of a complete new plant inside it. A spore falls off the plant and germinates. A male plant must fertilize a female plant to produce a new fern.

Gymnosperms

A gymnosperm is a vascular plant that produces seeds. The seeds rest in berries or cones. Seeds contain the beginnings of new plants called embryos. The seed provides protection and a source of food for the embryo. Seeds can travel long distances, allowing plants to spread to new areas.

The four main groups of gymnosperms are conifers, cycads, ginkgos, and gnetophytes. Most conifers are called evergreens because they keep their needle-like leaves all year long. Conifers are important in our daily lives. Most paper is made from conifer wood fibers.

Cycads look like palm trees and live mainly in tropical areas. Cycads produce cones instead of flowers. In some places, cycad seeds and trunks are used for food.

Ginkgos are attractive trees that resist many diseases and air pollution. Unlike other gymnosperms, ginkgo trees lose their leaves every year.

Gnetophytes are found in both very wet and very dry environments. Some species have unusual leather-like leaves that grow on vines. Other species resemble shrubs.

Gymnosperm Life Cycle

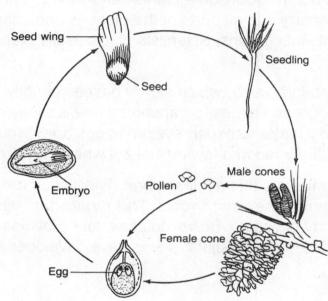

Angiosperms

An angiosperm is a vascular plant that produces flowers. The flowers make fruits to protect seeds. Like gymnosperms, angiosperms produce pollen. Bees often help spread pollen by carrying pollen on their legs from one flower to another.

A fruit is the part of a plant that contains the plant's fertilized seeds. All plants that produce flowers also produce fruit. You can eat many fruits, but not all fruits can be eaten. A cotton boll used to make cotton fabric is a fruit, but you would not eat it.

The life cycle of a fruiting plant has many steps. A seed sprouts and a new plant grows. The flower blooms and is pollinated. The flower is fertilized, and the petals fall off. The ovary grows and becomes the fruit. The fruit matures and protects the seeds inside.

Plant Adaptations

Plants have developed adaptations, or any part or characteristic that helps them survive or reproduce. Pine trees, for example, grow needle-like leaves with a waxy coating. This helps keep water in, so pines can survive in cool dry places.

How Are Plants Classified?

On the lines below, describe what happens to each term in the life cycle of a fruiting plant.

1. seed _____

_____

2. blooming flower _____

_____

3. fertilized flower _____

_____

4. ovary _____

_____

5. fruit _____

_____

Write *true* if the statement is true and *false* if the statement is false.

_____   **6.** Nonvascular plants absorb water like sponges.

_____   **7.** Vascular plants have tissues that act like sponges.

_____   **8.** For angiosperms, the flower is an essential part of the reproduction cycle.

9. Main Idea What are two main characteristics scientists use when classifying plants?

_____

_____

_____

10. Vocabulary Define *vascular* as it relates to plants.

_____

_____

11. Reading Skill: Compare and Contrast How are angiosperms and gymnosperms different?

_____

_____

_____

12. Critical Thinking: Evaluate Is the following statement accurate? "Plants produce fruits primarily to provide food for animals."

_____

_____

13. Inquiry Skill: Classify Would it be possible to identify a plant as either vascular or nonvascular by looking at tissues from the plant under a microscope?

_____

14. Test Prep Angiosperms are
   A nonflowering plants.
   B one-celled plants.
   C nonvascular plants.
   D flowering plants.

How Are Animals Classified?

The Animal Kingdom

The Kingdom Animalia is very varied. Some of these animals swim. Some fly, and many walk. Some do all of these things. There are animals that you can see only with a microscope. Others are as tall as a house. Humans belong to the animal kingdom. People share several characteristics with all animals.

Animals also have some of the same characteristics as organisms from other kingdoms. Like plants, animals have many cells. However, animals do not take in energy from the Sun as plants do. Animals take in food from their environment by eating. They break down and digest food for its energy and nutrients.

These are the most common characteristics used to classify animals: they have many cells, have tissues and organs, need oxygen to breathe, consume other organisms to get energy, are able to move, and reproduce sexually.

Invertebrates

An animal without a backbone is called an invertebrate. Invertebrates include the largest number of animal species. Invertebrates have different kinds of body symmetry, or a matching pattern. An organism can have bilateral symmetry, or matching form on opposite sides of an imaginary dividing line. There is also symmetry around a middle point, called radial symmetry.

There are six kinds of invertebrates. Cnidarians, like jellyfish, have mouths, the ability to eat food, and radial symmetry. Echinoderms, meaning "spiny skin," include sea urchins. They have radial symmetry and use sucker-like parts to catch prey. Sponges lack tissue and true body symmetry. Most live in the ocean.

Arthropods, including lobsters, crabs, spiders, and all insects, have body parts with movable joints and bilateral symmetry. This animal group has the most species.

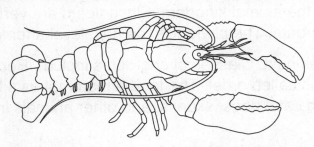

Mollusks include clams, oysters, snails, squids, and octopuses. They have soft bodies but can have hard shells. They move in different ways. Snails move slowly, but octopuses are very fast. Worms include groups such as flatworms and roundworms. They have bilateral symmetry and clearly defined heads.

Coldblooded Vertebrates

An animal that has a backbone is called a vertebrate. A backbone is a series of bones joined together with a flexible material called cartilage.

Some vertebrates are coldblooded, meaning their body temperature depends on the temperature outside their bodies. Low temperatures cool the animal's body. Warm temperatures heat it.

Fish are coldblooded vertebrates. Amphibians, such as frogs, toads, and salamanders, are coldblooded vertebrates that need to live near water but do not spend their entire lives in water.

Reptiles are coldblooded animals that have flexible, scaly skin that helps them keep water in their bodies. Snakes, turtles, tortoises, lizards, crocodiles, and alligators are reptiles.

Warmblooded Vertebrates

Birds and mammals are warmblooded animals. Their inside body temperature stays about the same all the time. Their cells produce enough heat to warm their bodies even when the outside temperature is low.

Birds are warmblooded. Birds are the only animal group that has feathers. Most birds can fly, but some do not.

Mammals are warmblooded animals that have many different organs and nervous systems that can do many different things. A mammal's brain is fairly large, so mammals can learn and do many things. All mammals have hair at some time in their lives.

Most mammals give birth to live young, to whom they feed milk. Mammals move on two legs or four legs, and some, like whales and dolphins, swim.

Classification System

To organize all the species, scientists divide the kingdoms into smaller groups. For example, tigers are members of the animal kingdom. Since tigers are vertebrates, they are members of the phylum Chordata. The phylum is the next level after kingdom.

A group called a class comes next. Classes of chordates include Reptilia, Amphibia, and Mammalia. The next group is called order. The food a mammal eats helps determine its order. Tigers are grouped with cats, dogs, skunks, and other animals in the order Carnivora.

Family and genus are the next levels. Animals in the same genus share many characteristics. Tigers belong to the same family and genus as lions. The most specific group is the species. Organisms of the same species are able to breed with each other. Tigers belong to the species *Panthera tigris*.

How Are Animals Classified?

Match each definition to its term.

Definitions

_____ **1.** organisms that do not have backbones

_____ **2.** a matching of form on both sides of an organism

_____ **3.** organisms whose body forms have radial symmetry, mouths, and the ability to eat food

_____ **4.** organisms that have a series of bones joined together with a flexible material called cartilage

_____ **5.** animals that usually need to live close to water, but do not spend their entire lives in water

Terms

a. amphibians

b. cnidarians

c. invertebrates

d. vertebrates

e. symmetry

Fill in the blanks to identify the class of vertebrates shown in each of the drawings below.

6. _____   **7.** _____   **8.** _____   **9.** _____

Write the answer to the question on the lines below.

10. How are the mammals different from other vertebrates?

_____

_____

_____

11. Main Idea Describe the diversity of the animal kingdom.

_____

_____

12. Vocabulary Define *invertebrate* and *vertebrate*. Compare the two groups of animals.

_____

_____

13. Reading Skill: Main Idea and Details Describe six different kinds of invertebrates.

_____

_____

_____

_____

_____

14. Critical Thinking: Synthesis What could you conclude if you observed an animal with feathers that couldn't fly? Is the animal a bird? Explain.

_____

_____

15. Inquiry Skill: Communicate Draw a chart or diagram on a separate sheet of paper to show how vertebrates are classified.

16. Test Prep Soft-bodied animals that may have a hard shell are called

   A sponges.

   B echinoderms.

   C mollusks.

   D mammals.

What Do Cells Do?

Plant Cells and Animal Cells

All living things are made of cells. All cells need food, water, and a way to eliminate wastes. A single cell is the smallest structure that carries out the activities necessary for life. Different structures in the cell do different things. One part gets food or water. Another part keeps the cell clean. Still other parts are in charge of reproduction. Like the parts of a factory, all parts of the cells must work together to run smoothly. An organism cannot survive without cells doing their work.

Animal cells and plants cells look different, but all cells have three parts: cell membrane, nucleus, and cytoplasm. The cell membrane is the outer covering of the cell. Water and food enter through the cell membrane, and wastes leave through it. Plant cells have an extra structure called the cell wall. The cell wall adds more support to a plant cell.

The nucleus is the control center for the cell. It directs all cell activities. The cytoplasm in animal and plant cells is a gel-like substance that surrounds all parts of the cell within the membrane. The cytoplasm contains the nucleus and the cell's organelles.

An organelle is a cell part with a particular job. Plants have special organelles called chloroplasts. Chloroplasts use energy from the Sun to combine water and carbon dioxide to make food for the cell.

Cell Transportation

The cell membrane holds matter inside but allows water, gases, and wastes to pass through it. In passive transport, matter moves into or out of the cell without using any of the cell's energy.

The simplest kind of passive transport is diffusion. Diffusion spreads substances through a gas or liquid. You can smell dinner across the room because food molecules diffuse through the air. Diffusion also transports many gases into and out of cells. Substances diffuse from areas with more matter to areas with less matter.

One special form of diffusion is called osmosis. Osmosis is the diffusion of water across a membrane. The membrane often stops many substances that are dissolved in the water. Osmosis keeps water inside cells.

Sometimes a cell needs to move materials opposite to the way diffusion would move them. In active transport, substances move from areas with less matter to areas with more matter. The cell must use energy to do this.

Large proteins in the cell membrane often help move materials in and out. The proteins act as tunnels that allow only certain materials to pass. Scientists study these proteins for clues to how the cell operates.

Using Energy

All living things need energy to survive. Plants use a process called photosynthesis to make food. This process takes place in chloroplasts and uses green pigment called chlorophyll to capture energy from sunlight.

During photosynthesis, chemical reactions join water with carbon dioxide. The byproducts are oxygen, which is released into the air, and glucose, or sugar, which the plant uses for food.

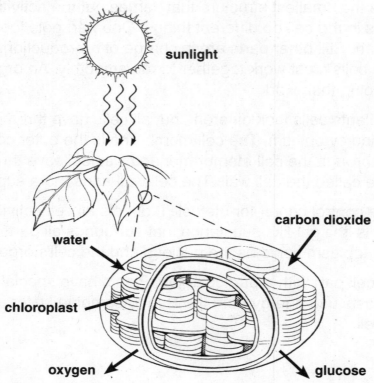

Plants and animals use organelles called mitochondria to break down sugars. Cells can use sugars as energy. Mitochondria perform cell respiration, the reverse reaction of photosynthesis. Glucose is combined with oxygen to form water and carbon dioxide. Energy is released. Mitochondria store this energy to be used later.

Cell Division

A human body is made of trillions of cells, but it began as just one cell. Cells can copy themselves through a process called cell division. New organisms begin when cells from two parents combine to form a new cell. The single cell divides into two cells. The two cells divide into four cells, and so on. As cells divide, they become different from each other. Early on, the cells organize themselves into three groups called germ layers. One layer will form the skin and nerves. Another layer becomes the lining of the digestive tract. The third layer produces all other body parts.

Bacteria and other single-celled organisms can also copy themselves. This copying results in new individuals. When conditions favor division, a bacterial colony can double very quickly.

What Do Cells Do?

Fill in the blanks.

1. The smallest structure that carries out all of the activities necessary for life is a(n) _____.

2. In both plant and animal cells, the _____ is the control center.

3. During the process of _____, substances are spread through a gas or a liquid.

4. _____ is a specialized form of diffusion, and diffusion is a type of passive transport.

5. During active transport, substances move from regions of _____ concentration to regions of _____ concentration.

6. The byproducts of photosynthesis are oxygen, which is released into the air, and a molecule called _____, a type of sugar.

7. Cells copy themselves in a process called _____.

8. Photosynthesis takes place in _____, which use energy from sunlight to make food in plants.

9. _____ perform a process the opposite of photosynthesis to help plants use energy as food.

animal cell 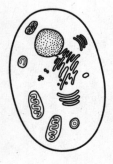    **plant cell**

10. Main Idea What do cells need to stay alive?

_____

_____

11. Vocabulary Use the terms *chloroplast* and *organelle* in a sentence that describes cell function.

_____

_____

12. Reading Skill: Draw Conclusions Could a cell survive without its mitochondria if all the other organelles were present?

_____

13. Critical Thinking: Analyze What are the parts of a cell? How do cell parts work together to keep the cell alive?

_____

_____

_____

_____

14. Inquiry Skill: Use Models Why is a drop of food coloring in water a good model for the process of diffusion?

_____

_____

15. Test Prep To make food, plants use a process called

   A photosynthesis.

   B cell division.

   C passive transport.

   D mitochondria.

How Are Cells Specialized?

Complex organisms have many types of cells. Each cell has special structures that allow it to carry out specific tasks.

Different Cells for Different Jobs

Organisms that have many cells have specialized cells that work together. A group of cells that has a common structure and function is called a tissue. Plants and animals have tissues that perform specific jobs.

Most complex organisms have a variety of tissues. Epithelial tissues are sheets of cells that cover surfaces and line certain body cavities and blood vessels. These tissues are usually smooth.

Connective tissue joins other tissues together. It also stores fat and makes blood cells. Bone, blood, and cartilage are types of connective tissue. Cartilage is the hard material inside your nose and outer ears.

Most animals use muscle tissues to move. Many muscles move together to move your body. Electrical impulses constantly run through your body and make muscles work. These impulses are produced in, and move through, nervous tissue. Nervous tissue can send signals throughout your body. Other nervous tissues protect nerves and provide them with nutrients.

Organs

Body functions like eating and walking are performed by special structures called organs. An organ is made up of several tissue types. These tissues work together to perform one or more functions. Some human organs are the brain, heart, and kidneys. Kidneys perform more than one function. They remove waste from the body and help control blood pressure.

Organ Systems

Organ systems are groups of organs that work together to perform complex tasks. The more complex an organism is, the more it needs a greater number of organ systems to carry out life processes. Humans have eleven organ systems. Each plays a particular role in your body. The systems also act on one another. Some organs work for more than one organ system.

One organ system is the circulatory system. This system carries oxygen to the body, removes carbon dioxide and other wastes, and helps keep your body temperature constant. The circulatory system includes your heart, arteries, and veins. At the kidneys, it connects to the urinary system. The urinary system helps control the amount of water and salt in the blood and removes liquid wastes.

The respiratory system brings oxygen into the body. The oxygen is then diffused into the blood. The respiratory system includes the lungs.

The muscular system and the skeletal system support all parts of your body and allow you to move. Bones and muscles make up these systems. Bones support muscles.

The brain is the center of the nervous system. All your senses feed information into the brain, which processes and responds to this information. The brain often sends signals down nerves to muscles. The brain also controls the other organ systems.

Your skin is also an organ system. The inside and outside layers of skin cells protect you from injury and keep in moisture. Three organ systems help your body fight infection and allow you to eat and reproduce. Another system produces hormones that control many body functions.

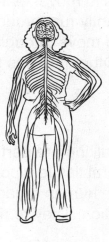

Brain and Nervous System

Endocrine System

Your body's endocrine system works like a chemical messenger system. The glands of the endocrine system act like communication centers. These glands make and send out hormones. A hormone acts as a message. It travels through the blood and is picked up only by certain cells.

Humans use about 50 different hormones. Some help to control growth and energy use. Others control blood sugar, minerals, and other chemicals. Some hormones cause specific changes in the body. For example, growth hormones cause dramatic changes in muscles and bones as you grow up. Growth hormones also influence when your growth will stop.

How Are Cells Specialized?

Fill in the blanks.

1. _____ are the communication centers in the endocrine system.

2. Smooth tissues that cover surfaces are _____.

3. Several tissues working together to perform one or more functions is a(n)

   _____.

4. Groups of organs that work together to perform a complex task are called

   _____.

5. _____ are chemical messages made by endocrine glands.

Circle the letter that best answers the question.

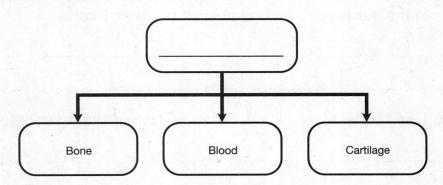

6. Which of the following words or phrases best completes the diagram above?

   A Epithelia   **C** Smooth Tissue

   B Connective Tissue **D** Organ Systems

7. What system controls the other organ systems?

   A circulatory   **C** respiratory

   B nervous   **D** endocrine

8. Main Idea What are specialized cells?

_____

_____

9. Vocabulary Define *tissue*. Use this word in a sentence that describes how organisms accomplish tasks.

_____

_____

10. Reading Skill: Main Idea and Details Describe the interaction between two human organ systems that work together.

_____

_____

_____

11. Critical Thinking: Evaluate Would it be accurate to say that all multicellular organisms have the same type and number of organs? Explain.

_____

_____

_____

12. Inquiry Skill: Use Models How is the nervous system like a set of telephone wires?

_____

_____

13. Test Prep The brain is part of the

   A muscular system.

   B urinary system.

   C circulatory system.

   D nervous system.

How Do Oxygen and Carbon Dioxide Cycle?

Photosynthesis and Respiration

Organisms use oxygen and carbon dioxide over and over. Some of this cycling happens during photosynthesis and respiration. A runner breathes faster and more deeply as she runs because her body needs more oxygen. Green plants and algae make most of the oxygen in the atmosphere.

Plants and algae make oxygen and food through photosynthesis. During photosynthesis, energy from the Sun is used to change carbon dioxide and water into a simple sugar called glucose and oxygen.

Glucose gives plants energy, which is stored inside food. Animals get the energy when they eat the plants. Animals that eat other animals also get energy from glucose. The oxygen is released into the atmosphere.

Most organisms are able to use the chemical energy in food through respiration. During respiration, oxygen joins with glucose to produce carbon dioxide and water. The stored energy is let go.

Plants, animals, and many other organisms carry out respiration. Respiration is why oxygen is so important to life on Earth, including human life. You take in oxygen with every breath. Your blood carries oxygen to the cells in your body, where respiration is always taking place.

Photosynthesis and respiration work in opposite ways. The things that are used during photosynthesis (carbon dioxide and water) are produced during respiration. The things that are used during respiration (oxygen and glucose) are produced during photosynthesis. This is how oxygen and carbon dioxide cycle through the biosphere.

Just as animals need plants for food and oxygen, plants need animals for carbon dioxide.

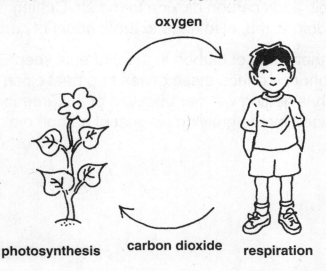

oxygen

photosynthesis   carbon dioxide   respiration

Carbon Cycle and Oxygen Cycle

Carbon is one of Earth's most common elements—materials that cannot be broken down into other materials. It is a basic part of all living things. Carbon is part of every body cell, every sugar, and carbon dioxide gas. Carbon is also part of Earth's outer layer called the crust. Much carbon is underground in fossil fuels such as coal, oil, and natural gas.

Carbon moves through the carbon cycle mostly as carbon dioxide gas. Plants take in carbon dioxide during photosynthesis, and it goes into molecules like glucose. When organisms use the glucose, carbon goes back into the environment as carbon dioxide.

Carbon also moves through the environment in other ways. When organisms die, some carbon stays in their bodies. As bacteria and fungi break down dead organisms, carbon leaves their bodies and returns to the environment. Burning fossil fuels also moves carbon back into the environment.

Living things need oxygen to live. Like carbon, oxygen cycles through the environment. Oxygen is produced during photosynthesis. Some oxygen comes from water vapor in the atmosphere. Oxygen is used during respiration. It is also consumed when metals rust or when something burns.

Because oxygen is one of the substances that make up carbon dioxide, the oxygen cycle is tied to the carbon cycle. Both carbon and oxygen cycle between living and nonliving things in the environment.

Things that happen on Earth can change or harm the carbon and oxygen cycles. When people cut down trees in the rain forests, there is less photosynthesis. This means that less oxygen enters the atmosphere and less carbon dioxide leaves.

Disrupting the Cycle

Each year there is more carbon dioxide in the atmosphere. Burning fossil fuels, such as natural gas, coal, and oil, adds carbon dioxide to the air. Cutting down trees, such as when the rain forests are deforested, also adds to the amount of carbon dioxide.

Carbon dioxide and other kinds of carbon in the air helps keep Earth warm. Through a process called the greenhouse effect, these gases trap heat close to Earth's surface. Many scientists think Earth is getting warmer because of the greenhouse effect. The environment can be damaged by the growing amount of carbon dioxide.

How Do Oxygen and Carbon Dioxide Cycle?

Write answers to the questions on the lines below.

> carbon dioxide + water + energy ➡ glucose + oxygen

1. What process is shown in the diagram above?

2. What happens during this process?

   _____

   _____

> glucose + oxygen ➡ carbon dioxide + water + energy

3. What process is shown in the diagram above?

   _____

4. What happens during this process?

   _____

   _____

5. What are two causes of the increase in carbon dioxide in the atmosphere?

   _____

© Houghton Mifflin Harcourt Publishing Company Core Skills Science, G6 SV 9781419098468

6. **Main Idea** How do living things depend on the carbon dioxide cycle and the oxygen cycle?

_____

_____

7. **Vocabulary** Write a sentence that relates the terms *photosynthesis* and *respiration*.

_____

_____

8. **Reading Skill: Compare and Contrast** Contrast the processes of photosynthesis and respiration.

_____

_____

9. **Critical Thinking: Evaluate** Will the amount of carbon dioxide in the atmosphere soon be greater than the amount of oxygen? Explain.

_____

_____

10. **Inquiry Skill: Predict** You blow through a straw into a beaker of water that has algae growing in it. If you then cover the container, will the level of carbon dioxide increase or decrease over time? Explain your answer.

_____

_____

11. **Test Prep** Which process provides the oxygen you breathe?

    A greenhouse effect

    B deforestation

    C respiration

    D photosynthesis

How Do Nitrogen and Water Cycle?

Most of Earth's water is in the oceans. Most of the nitrogen is a gas in the air. Living things use both water and nitrogen, which cycle between Earth's surface and atmosphere.

Nitrogen in the Environment

Much of Earth's atmosphere is made of nitrogen gas. But most plants and animals need nitrogen in the form of nitrogen compounds in order to use it. During nitrogen fixation, nitrogen gas is changed into useful nitrogen compounds.

Lightning helps with nitrogen fixation. The energy from lightning joins nitrogen and oxygen in the air. The new compounds mix with rainwater.

Most nitrogen fixation is done by special bacteria that live in soil, water, and on the roots of some plants. The roots feed the bacteria, and the bacteria give the plants fixed nitrogen.

Organisms called decomposers keep plants and animals from using all the nitrogen. Decomposers such as bacteria and fungi break down, or decompose, animal wastes and dead plants and animals. This puts nitrogen compounds back into the soil, so plants can use them. Other bacteria change nitrogen in the soil into the nitrogen gas in the air.

Sometimes people do things that leave too much or too little nitrogen in the soil. This upsets the nitrogen cycle. When farmers cut down plants that are used for food, the nitrogen in the plants goes away and does not come back. Water can also wash nitrogen out of the soil. Farmers put chemicals called fertilizers on the soil to add nitrogen back in. They also plant peanuts or beans because nitrogen-fixing bacteria live on their roots.

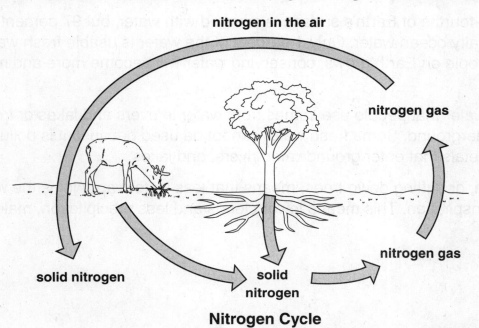

nitrogen in the air

nitrogen gas

nitrogen gas

solid nitrogen

solid nitrogen

Nitrogen Cycle

Water in the Environment

The bodies of all living things are made mostly of water. Living things need water so their life processes can work. Like oxygen and carbon dioxide, water cycles through the environment.

Most of Earth's water is found in oceans. Ocean water is salty. Fresh water is found in lakes, rivers, and other bodies of water. Some of the water on land is under the ground in the soil or in spaces between solid rocks. Frozen water makes up snow, ice, and large pieces of snow and ice called glaciers. Water in the atmosphere is water vapor and tiny drops of water or ice in clouds.

The Water Cycle

Water is always moving from Earth's surface to Earth's atmosphere and back to the surface in a process called the water cycle. Energy from the Sun heats up water in the oceans and on land. During evaporation, water uses this energy to change from a liquid to a gas called water vapor. Water evaporates from a plant's leaves during a process called transpiration.

Animals are also part of the water cycle. They give off water as urine, sweat, and as water vapor when they breathe. Any liquid water animals give off evaporates.

Water vapor in the atmosphere can condense, or turn into a liquid. Tiny drops of water form clouds. When the drops of water get heavy, they fall to Earth as rain, sleet, hail, or snow. Water that falls to Earth from a cloud is called precipitation.

Water Conservation

Almost three-fourths of Earth's surface is covered with water, but 97 percent of Earth's water is salty ocean water. Only 1 percent of the water is usable fresh water. As the number of people on Earth grows, conserving water will become more and more important.

Most of the water that people use comes from water in rivers and lakes or from water that is stored underground. Some fresh water cannot be used because it is polluted by chemicals and metals that enter groundwater, rivers, and lakes.

Deforestation, or cutting down trees, means that less water vapor joins the water cycle through transpiration. This means fewer clouds and less precipitation, making these places drier.

How Do Nitrogen and Water Cycle?

Fill in the blanks.

1. The process of changing nitrogen gas into usable nitrogen is called

   _____.

2. As a result of _____, nitrogen compounds return to the soil.

Label the steps of the water cycle in the diagram below.

4. _____

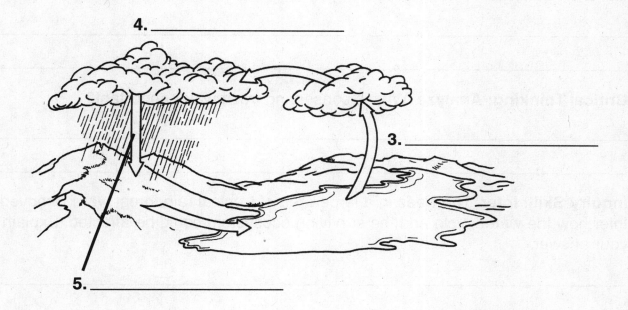

3. _____

5. _____

6. Of the 3 percent of Earth's water that is not salt water, less than _____ is usable fresh water.

7. Available fresh water is limited by _____, particularly by metals and chemicals.

8. Main Idea Why is the cycling of nitrogen and water so important for life?

_____

_____

9. Vocabulary Explain the difference between evaporation and transpiration.

_____

_____

10. Reading Skill: Main Idea and Details What process makes nitrogen usable by plants and animals? What are two ways this process takes place?

_____

_____

11. Critical Thinking: Analyze Why is conserving fresh water important?

_____

_____

12. Inquiry Skill: Infer The trees in a large area of tropical rain forest were removed. Infer how the water cycle and the surviving ecosystem could be affected. Explain your answer.

_____

_____

_____

13. Test Prep Nitrogen gas in the air can be used by

  A most plants.

  B certain animals.

  C certain bacteria.

  D all organisms.

What Are Earth's Ecosystems?

Community Interactions

Living things need one another. They also need nonliving things, such as air, water, and soil. An ecosystem is made up of all the living and non-living things in an area. The living parts of an ecosystem, such as animals, plants, and microorganisms, are called its biotic factors. The nonliving parts of an ecosystem are called its abiotic factors. These include temperature, precipitation, wind, soil, and other nonliving things. The biotic factors depend on each other and on the abiotic factors to say alive.

Abiotic factors that support life are found nearly everywhere on Earth. These factors vary from place to place, which means that ecosystems and the life they support vary, too. One important abiotic factor is climate.

Living things survive in many different ecosystems. Living things depend on an ecosystem's climate to survive. Climate is the average weather in a place from year to year. Climate affects the kinds of things that live in an ecosystem.

Montana is cooler than Florida because it is farther north of the equator. Its climate is called temperate, which means it is warm in the summer and cold in the winter. Places with temperate climates do not have as much precipitation as tropical places.

Fewer living things survive in the wild areas of Montana than in Florida. That is because Montana's colder, temperate climate makes it harder for all organisms to live there.

Land Biomes

Most species live best in their own biome. A biome is a large group of similar ecosystems. It has similar climates and living things. The six main land biomes are tundra, taiga, grassland, temperate forest, tropical rain forest, and desert.

The tundra is a cold biome with no trees. A thick layer of ice called permafrost stays below the soil all year. Mosses and shrubs can grow here. Arctic foxes, musk oxen, and snowy owls live here. They have thick coats of fur or feathers to help them survive the cold.

The taiga is an evergreen forest biome just south of the tundra. It is warmer and wetter than the tundra. Ferns and mosses, along with grasses and flowers, grow here.

Birds, squirrels, and bears live in the taiga. All summer, they store food and fat for the cold winter. They have thick coats to keep them warm.

In grasslands, there is enough rain for grasses to survive but not trees. Grasslands are found on every continent except Antarctica and can be very cold, very hot, or temperate. Most grasslands have wet and dry seasons.

Grassland animals and plants must be able to survive without water during dry seasons. Plants must be able to grow back from their roots after fires. The animals must be able to run fast or hide to survive.

Plants and animals live easily in temperate forests because there is much rainfall and sunlight. Their winters are not as cold as in the taiga, and their summers are warmer. This biome has trees, grasses, ferns, and bushes. Many insects, reptiles, birds, and mammals live in it. Animal adaptations include thick fur coats, hibernation, and migration.

Warm, wet tropical rain forests are found close to the equator. Because of the warm temperatures and high amount of rainfall, many species of animals and plants live here. This means that this biome has great biodiversity.

Rain forest organisms work hard to get sunlight, find food, and stay safe. Trees grow taller than other plants to reach sunlight. Many animals have adaptations to help them find food and stay safe. For example, some frogs have poison in their skin to keep enemies away. Monkeys use long tails and fingers to climb trees for food and safety.

Deserts are places that get little or no rainfall. Only strong living things survive in this biome using special adaptations. Animals find water in seeds they eat. They stay cool by hiding during the day. They hunt at night when it is cooler. Cactuses store water inside their tissues. Their thorns help keep them from being eaten by animals.

Ocean Biome

Water covers almost three-quarters of Earth's surface. Water biomes include freshwater biomes and saltwater biomes like the oceans.

Different areas of the ocean are called zones. Each zone has different characteristics. Organisms in each zone have adapted to become the right life forms for those conditions.

The intertidal zone is the area right along the shore that water reaches when the tide goes in and out. In the neritic zone, the water is shallow and filled with nutrients. Crabs, shrimp, and fish live here. The open sea is the oceanic zone. Most organisms in this zone live at the top of the ocean where there is more sunlight. Only organisms that have adapted to the dark, cold water live in the deep ocean.

What Are Earth's Ecosystems?

1. What are some of the biotic factors of an ecosystem?

   _____

2. What are some abiotic factors in an ecosystem?

   _____

3. What is a climate?

   _____

4. What is a biome?

   _____

5. What is the difference between tundra and taiga?

   _____

6. What is the difference between grasslands and temperate forests?

   _____

   _____

Label the zones in the diagram below.

7. _____   8. _____   9. _____

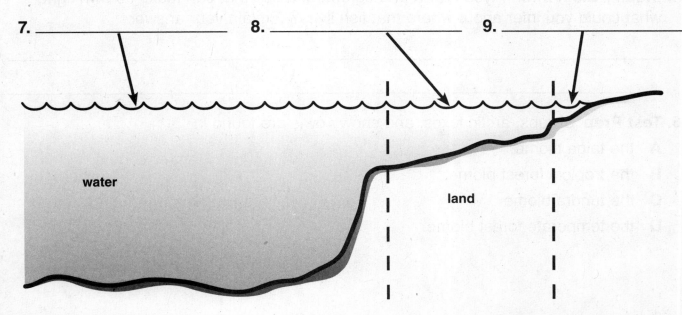

water

land

10. Main Idea Explain how the abiotic factors in an ecosystem determine the types of organisms living there. Use a desert biome as an example.

_____

_____

11. Vocabulary Define *biodiversity*. Explain which biome has the greatest biodiversity and why.

_____

_____

_____

12. Reading Skill: Cause and Effect Explain why different ocean zones are home to very different species.

_____

_____

13. Critical Thinking: Evaluation Based on the adaptations of animals, evaluate what might happen to the animals in a biome if Earth's temperature increased.

_____

_____

14. Inquiry Skill: Infer If you saw a photograph of a fish that can make its own light, what could you infer about where that fish lives? Explain your answer.

_____

_____

15. Test Prep Shrubs, arctic foxes, and snowy owls are found in

  A the taiga biome.

  B the tropical forest biome.

  C the tundra biome.

  D the temperate forest biome.

What Roles Do Species Play?

Niche

Every organism in an ecosystem has its own niche, or role, in that ecosystem. A species' niche is its relationship with the biotic and abiotic factors in the ecosystem. A niche includes where a species lives and how it cares for its offspring.

Part of an animal's niche depends on what it eats and what eats it. A predator is an animal that eats other animals. The prey is the animal that is eaten.

Some species are generalists. They fit into a large niche. For example, raccoons are predators that eat almost anything. They dine on nuts, birds, and even garbage!

Other species are specialists and occupy a very specific niche. For example, five different insect-eating birds called wood warblers live in evergreen forests and hunt in the same trees. But each warbler works in a different part of the tree. They also make nests and raise their young at different times.

Food Webs

Energy and nutrients transfer, or move, from plants to animals. A food chain shows how energy moves from producers to consumers. A group of overlapping food chains forms a food web. A food web shows how energy is transferred in an ecosystem.

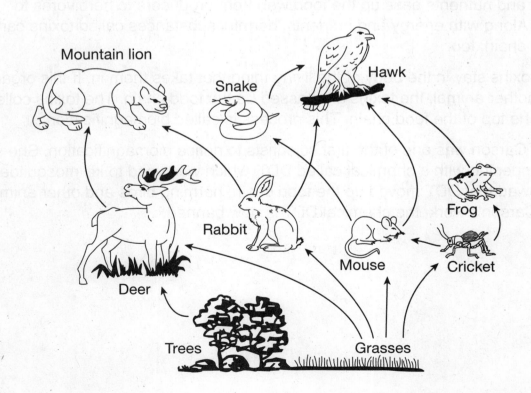

All food webs have the same parts: producers, herbivores, carnivores, omnivores, and decomposers. These parts are organized in the same way.

Producers, like plants and algae, are at the bottom of the food web. They use the Sun's energy to make food. This energy passes to herbivores, or plant-eating animals. Herbivores, like deer and rabbits, are primary consumers, the first animals in any food chain.

Animals that get their energy from eating herbivores are called carnivores. Carnivores, including hawks, rattlesnakes, and lions, are consumers. Omnivores get energy from eating plants and animals. Carnivores and omnivores are at the top of a food web.

Decomposers are animals that eat dead plants and animals. They break down the dead things into nutrients for the soil. In every ecosystem, nutrients move from plants to animals to decomposers and back to plants.

The top carnivore plays an important role in most ecosystems. If this animal, such as a lion, is healthy, it shows the ecosystem is healthy. Top carnivores cannot survive without healthy plants and animal populations below them.

In healthy ecosystems, the population of each species should stay large enough to reproduce. It should also stay small enough for the species to have enough food.

Biomagnification

Energy and nutrients pass up the food web from producers to herbivores to carnivores. Along with energy and nutrients, harmful substances called toxins can pass up the food chain, too.

Some toxins stay in the body of the living thing that takes them in. If this organism is eaten by another animal, the toxins are passed up the food chain. The toxins collect in animals at the top of the food chain. This process is called biomagnification.

Rachel Carson was one of the first scientists to notice biomagnification. She saw this problem happening with a chemical called DDT, which was used to kill mosquitoes. Carson showed that DDT moved up the food chain, harming birds and other animals. Thanks to Carson's work, the chemical DDT is now banned.

What Roles Do Species Play?

Write answers to the questions on the lines below.

1. What is a species' niche?

   _____

   _____

2. How does the presence of top carnivores indicate that an ecosystem is healthy?

   _____

   _____

   _____

3. Why are raccoons called a generalist species?

   _____

Fill in the blanks.

4. _____ are at the bottom of the food web.

5. _____ and omnivores are found at the top of the food web.

6. Animals that break down dead things into nutrients that go into soil are

   _____ .

7. Main Idea Explain how each species in an ecosystem depends on other species.

_____

_____

8. Vocabulary How is a carnivore different from an omnivore?

_____

_____

9. Reading Skill: Classify Classify each of the following species as producers, herbivores, carnivores, or omnivores: deer, raccoon, oak tree, rabbit, cactus, grass, rattlesnake.

_____

_____

10. Critical Thinking: Apply Which of the following species would you expect to be most vulnerable to biomagnification: hawk, bumblebee, oak tree, deer, or raccoon? Explain your answer.

_____

_____

11. Inquiry Skill: Measure Suppose you wanted to measure the amount of DDT in a food chain. Which animals in the food chain would you measure? Explain your strategy.

_____

_____

_____

12. Test Prep A niche is

   A a type of forest biome.

   B a type of tropical bird.

   C the part of a food web occupied by a top predator.

   D the specific role of a species in an ecosystem.

What Limits Population Growth?

Limited Resources

The population of a species depends on resources such as food and water. A limiting factor is something that stops a population from growing or spreading out. Limiting factors can be things animals need, such as water, food, and space. Limiting factors can also be competition, predation, illness, and humans. Without limiting factors, populations would keep getting larger.

Competition

Competition is the struggle among living things to use the same resources in an ecosystem. Sometimes the competition is between members of the same species. Plants, for example, might compete for space to grow. There is also competition between different species. Owls and hawks might compete for the same prey.

Ecosystem Balance

Limiting factors control the numbers of organisms an ecosystem can support. This number is called the carrying capacity. An ecosystem is in balance when the carrying capacity is reached for all its species.

Predators

When a predator catches and eats a prey, predation is taking place. For example, many wolves eat deer. When the prey population of deer grows, wolves have plenty to eat. The wolf population grows, and the deer population goes down. Now that the wolves' main food resource is diminished, the wolf population gets smaller, too. With fewer predator wolves, the deer population begins to grow again. Then the predator-prey cycle repeats.

Predator and prey species can live together this way for a long time. Their population numbers cycle from high to low to high, naturally controlling the population.

wolf: predator    **deer: prey**

Diseases

A disease is something that stops an organism's body from working. It is an important limiting factor because it can stop population growth. Diseases can affect animal populations weakened by overcrowding or lack of food and water. Plant populations can also suffer from disease. Dutch elm disease killed most elm trees in the United States between 1930 and the 1970s.

Invasive Species

Invasive species are plants or animals that are not native to an ecosystem. When these organisms enter a balanced ecosystem, they can cause many problems. Because they have no natural enemies, their populations can grow quickly. They also use up resources such as food, water, and space. They can destroy habitats and disrupt the food chain.

Extinction

Most of the species that ever lived on Earth are now extinct. Extinction is the complete disappearance of a species. Extinction can happen when an ecosystem changes. A food source might be lost, predators might increase, or disease might appear.

Many species become extinct naturally, but humans have brought invasive species to places and caused native species to become extinct. The most significant way humans cause extinction is by destroying habitats and using up natural resources.

Rescuing Species

Many people now work to stop species from becoming extinct. In the United States, laws protect plants and animals that are close to extinction.

Captive breeding is one way to help animals close to extinction. During captive breeding, animals live and reproduce in controlled habitats with plenty of resources. Captive breeding helps the population of a species get larger. Then the species is placed back into the wild. Captive breeding saved the California condor, pictured below, from extinction.

What Limits Population Growth?

Fill in the blanks in the diagram below to give examples of limiting factors.

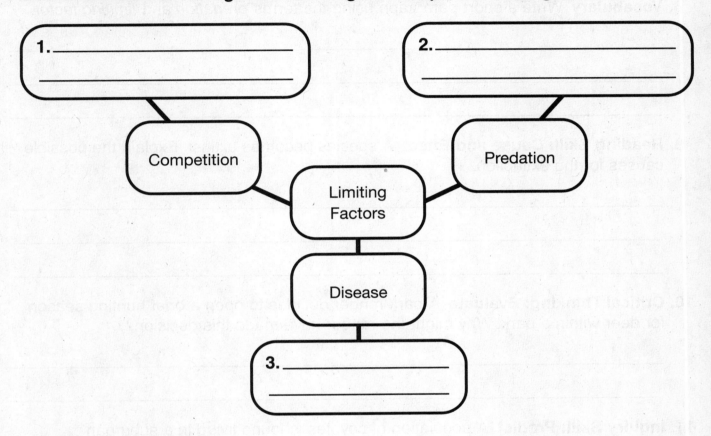

1. _____

2. _____

Competition

Predation

Limiting
Factors

Disease

3. _____

Write *true* if the statement is true and *false* if the statement is false.

_____ 4. The natural balance of ecosystems cannot be destroyed by invasive species.

_____ 5. The most significant way that humans increase the rate of extinction is through habitat destruction.

_____ 6. Most of the species that ever lived on Earth are now extinct.

7. Main Idea What type of population will be most vulnerable to disease?

_____

8. Vocabulary Write a short paragraph using the terms *predation* and *limiting factor*.

_____

_____

_____

9. Reading Skill: Cause and Effect A species becomes extinct. Explain the possible causes for the extinction.

_____

_____

_____

_____

10. Critical Thinking: Evaluate A park ranger decides to open a brief hunting season for deer within a park. Why might the ranger have made this decision?

_____

_____

_____

11. Inquiry Skill: Predict A population of coyotes is found living in a suburban neighborhood. Over time, what will happen to the number of coyotes in the neighborhood? Explain your answer.

_____

_____

_____

12. Test Prep Which of the following is NOT a limiting factor?

   A disease

   B competition

   C predation

   D extinction

What Are the Three Classes of Rock?

Rocks can be grouped into three classes depending on how they are formed. Over time, heat and pressure can change rock from one class to another.

What Is Rock?

Rocks are mixtures of two or more minerals. The way a rock looks tells you something about how it formed. Granite has grains of different minerals. Other rocks look as if they were made out of clay, sand, or even shells. The properties of a rock depend in part on the properties of the minerals it has in it.

Rocks of the same kind can have different grain sizes and textures. Some rocks have bands or stripes. A rock's physical features can help you understand how that rock was formed and find out what kind of rock it is. Geologists are scientists who can tell us much about Earth and its history by studying rocks and minerals.

Igneous Rock

Melted rock beneath the Earth's surface is called magma. As magma cools beneath the Earth's surface, it hardens into igneous rocks. Granite is a type of igneous rock formed from cooled magma.

Minerals with higher melting points crystallize first. Minerals with lower melting points crystallize next. If magma cools quickly, small crystals form. Some magma may take thousands of years to cool, which creates very large crystals. Magma that reaches the Earth's surface is called lava.

Sedimentary Rock

Sedimentary rock is formed from sediment, or broken-down rocks, minerals, sand, and mud. Over millions of years, thick layers of sediment build up. The weight of the layers squeezes out the water and forms rock.

Different kinds of rock form different kinds of sediment. Smooth mud turns into shale. Grains of quartz in sand become sandstone. Limestone forms from the shells of corals and ocean animals. You can often find fossils of sea animals in limestone.

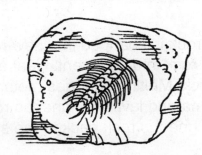

Metamorphic Rock

The term *metamorphose* means to change form. Rock can change form when it is pressed under great pressure or heated to a high temperature. Rock that is formed by changes is metamorphic rock. Any kind of rock can turn into metamorphic rock.

The high temperatures and pressure deep beneath the Earth's surface make buried rocks softer. This change can affect the texture and mineral composition of the rock. New minerals may form new rock. Gneiss is metamorphic rock.

Weathering and Erosion

Earth's features are always changing. Most of these changes happen slowly over millions of years. Wind, rain, and ice break down rock and move sediment. Rivers carve out deep canyons. Chemical processes dissolve minerals. Living things also break down rock. The growing roots of plants can crack the top layers of bedrock. The wearing away of rock is called weathering. The moving of sediment is called erosion.

Weathering smoothes the edges of rocks and wears down the peaks of mountains. Over millions of years, these changes affect all of Earth's land features. They also help create new rock.

The Rock Cycle

The process through which rock is changed into new rock is called the rock cycle. Weathering and erosion change rock into sediment. Heat and pressure change any type of rock into metamorphic rock. Melting changes metamorphic rock into magma and lava. Cooling changes magma and lava into igneous rock. Earth movements uplift sedimentary, metamorphic, and igneous rock back to the surface of Earth. The rock cycle then begins again.

Name _____ Date _____

What Are the Three Classes of Rocks?

Circle the letter that best answers the question or completes the sentence.

1. When magma cools, minerals with higher melting points will

   A crystallize first.   **C** turn into metamorphic rock.

   B crystallize second.   **D** fill in the gaps.

2. What processes impact all of Earth's land features and play a part in creating new rock?

   A metamorphism and transporting

   B weathering and erosion

   C folding and banding

   D cooling and stacking

3. What is the rock cycle?

   A the process of breaking away rock and then depositing it

   B the process of magma cooling and crystallizing into new rock

   C the process of rock changing into new rock in different ways

   D the process of a volcano erupting magma onto Earth's surface

Label the steps in each part of the rock cycle.

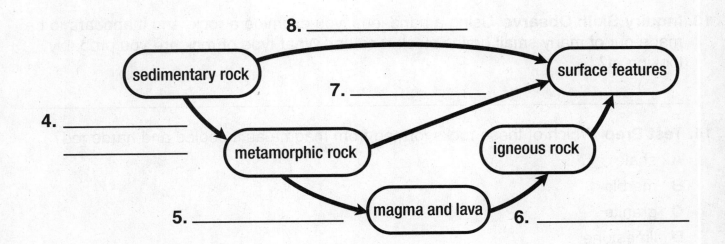

8. _____

sedimentary rock

7. _____

surface features

4. _____
   _____

metamorphic rock

igneous rock

5. _____

magma and lava

6. _____

9. **Main Idea** Describe how igneous rocks are formed.

_____

10. **Vocabulary** Write a brief paragraph using the terms *sedimentary rock*, *metamorphic rock*, and *rock cycle*.

_____

_____

_____

11. **Reading Skill: Compare and Contrast** Compare and contrast the steps in the formation of igneous rocks with large crystals and igneous rocks with small crystals.

_____

_____

_____

12. **Critical Thinking: Analyze** A rock formation has layers of shale and limestone. What can be inferred about the changes that the landscape has gone through?

_____

_____

_____

13. **Inquiry Skill: Observe** Using a hand lens, you examine a rock, and it appears to be made out of many small grains stuck together. What type of rock are you probably looking at?

_____

_____

14. **Test Prep** Which of these rocks formed from magma as it cooled and hardened?

A shale

B marble

C granite

D limestone

What Are Tectonic Plates?

Moving Plates

Earth's continents have not always been in the places where they are today. They once existed as one great landmass called Pangaea.

Scientists believe Pangaea split into two large parts. One of the parts is called Gondwanaland. It was made up of the southern continents—South America, Africa, Australia, and Antarctica—as well as India and several islands. The second part, Laurasia, was made up of the northern continents—North America, Europe, and Asia—as well as several islands, including Greenland and the British Isles. Both Gondwanaland and Laurasia split again, eventually forming the continents of today.

How do continents move around Earth? To answer, you need to understand the inside of Earth.

Earth's Layers

Earth is made up of four main layers. From the surface inward, these layers are the crust, mantle, outer core, and inner core. The continents are part of Earth's thin outer layer called the crust. Under the crust is a thick layer called the mantle. The mantle is made of heavy rock. The crust and the upper part of the mantle form a stiff rocky layer called the lithosphere. The lithosphere is broken up into pieces called tectonic plates.

LAYERS OF EARTH

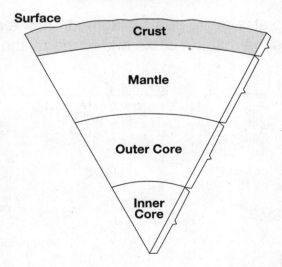

The part of the mantle just under the lithosphere is warmer and softer than the layers above it. Tectonic plates float on this layer. At the center of Earth is the core. The outer core is liquid, and the inner core is solid. Both cores are made mostly of iron.

Scientists have found seven major plates and many smaller plates. The line between one plate and another is called a plate boundary. The plates can be all ocean crust or both ocean and continental crust. The tectonic plates and the continents on them both move. The study of these movements and the changes in Earth's surface that they cause is called plate tectonics.

What makes the plates move? One idea suggests that hot, soft rock in the mantle below the plates is moving slowly in huge loops called convection cells. These cells move the plates.

Sea-Floor Spreading

Underwater mountain chains are called mid-ocean ridges. These ridges are part of all Earth's oceans. They mark the areas where two plates are moving apart. Mid-ocean ridges are connected across Earth.

In the center of these ridges are deep valleys, called rift valleys. As the rifts spread apart, magma flows up and fills the space. This action is called sea-floor spreading.

The discovery of sea-floor spreading gives evidence to support plate tectonics. First, it explains how plates grow and shrink. If one plate is growing, another must be shrinking. Second, the oldest ocean floor sediment is only about 200 million years old—far younger than Earth. The ocean floor is youngest next to the rift valley and becomes older farther away. At places where plates come together, the floor is being destroyed.

A plate is destroyed where one plate moves beneath another. The sinking plate goes down into the mantle, where it melts and is recycled. New plates are created when a landmass splits apart.

Plates grow when two plates move apart. Magma from the mantle rises up through the crack between them. As the magma cools and hardens, the new rock becomes part of the plates.

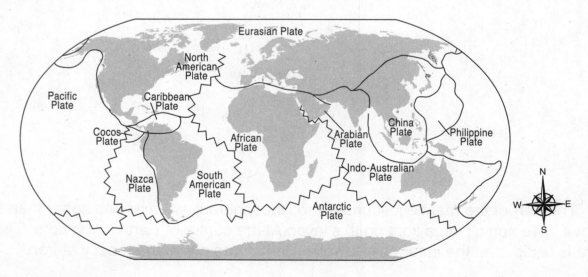

Name _____ Date _____

What Are Tectonic Plates?

1. The Earth's thin outer layer is called the _____.

2. The tectonic plates are part of the _____.

3. The _____ is made of heavy rock.

4. The _____ is a liquid layer at the center of the Earth.

5. The solid layer at the center of the Earth is called the _____.

Write *true* if the statement is true and *false* if the statement is false.

_____ **6.** Scientists have discovered seven major tectonic plates and many smaller plates.

_____ **7.** The theory of plate tectonics is the study of how Earth's surface has remained the same for billions of years.

_____ **8.** Plates are enlarged where one plate moves beneath another, and they are destroyed when two plates move apart.

_____ **9.** The mid-ocean ridges mark the areas where two plates are moving apart, and these ridges are connected across Earth.

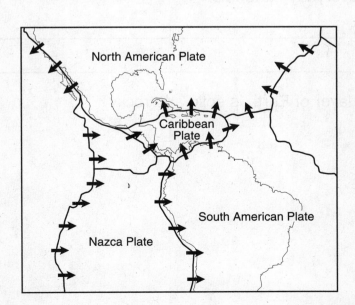

10. Main Idea What is one idea explaining how tectonic plates move on Earth's surface?

_____

11. Vocabulary Write a sentence using the terms *lithosphere* and *crust*.

_____

_____

12. Reading Skill: Main Idea and Details In one or two sentences, summarize the main idea of the *Sea-Floor Spreading* section.

_____

_____

_____

_____

13. Critical Thinking: Synthesis How does sea-floor spreading alter the shape of the ocean floor?

_____

_____

_____

14. Inquiry Skill: Use Models Describe how you would create a model of sea-floor spreading, using everyday materials.

_____

_____

_____

15. Test Prep Which layer of Earth is solid and rocky?

   A outer core

   B lithosphere

   C mantle

   D inner core

What Changes Do Moving Plates Cause?

Plate Boundaries

Have you noticed that the West Coast of the United States has many earthquakes? In addition, a huge ocean wave called a tsunami sometimes reaches the shores of Hawaii and other Pacific Ocean coastlines. Most of the time earthquakes under the ocean floor cause these waves. Why do some places have such dangerous events while other places are safer from them?

The edges of Earth's tectonic plates are called plate boundaries. Earth's lithosphere is broken up into large pieces that move over the upper mantle. Movement and contact between these plates cause earthquakes, volcanoes, and other Earth events and structures. There are three types of plate boundaries: convergent, divergent, and transform fault.

Convergent boundaries form where two plates push together. If both plates are made of continental crust, the land crumples into high mountains like the Himalayas. If one plate is made of oceanic crust, it sinks below the other plate. If two oceanic plates converge, one plate usually sinks below the other and forms a trench. Volcanoes and earthquakes generally happen along sinking plate boundaries.

Divergent boundaries form where plates move apart. This generally happens along mid-ocean ridges. Magma rises through the rift, creating new crust that forms underwater mountains. These mountains are often as tall as the mountains on Earth's surface. Volcanoes and earthquakes often happen along the underwater ridges.

Transform fault boundaries form where two plates are sliding past each other. A fault is a crack in Earth's crust caused by the sliding plates. Most transform fault boundaries form along the mid-ocean ridges. However, the well-known San Andreas fault runs along the coast of California. California sits on two tectonic plates! Part of California is on the Pacific Plate, while the rest of California is on the North American Plate.

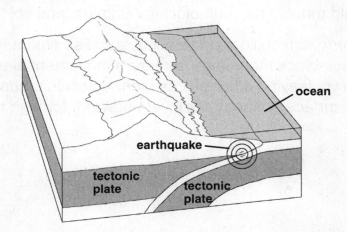

ocean

earthquake

tectonic plate

tectonic plate

Earthquakes

An earthquake is the most common Earth event that happens along a transform fault boundary. This is because the edge of the boundary is not smooth. Sections of the fault get caught up or locked along edges of the boundary that are not smooth. Stresses build along this area as the plates slide past each other.

Eventually the stresses become too great, and the rock moves very quickly, causing an earthquake. The place where the movement first happens is called the focus. It is usually along a plate boundary deep beneath Earth's surface. The point on the surface above the focus is called the epicenter, where shaking is often the greatest.

The shaking is caused by energy released when the rock moves. The energy is carried by seismic waves, which spread out from the focus in all directions. The waves become weaker as they travel away from the focus. Seismic waves can cause buildings and roads to collapse, which can kill people.

Volcanoes

Volcanoes form when magma is pushed to the surface through weak places in Earth's crust. Such places include faults, plate boundaries, and "hot spots" where magma has melted the rock above it.

During an eruption, magma rises through one or more vents. It then comes out as lava on the surface. Most lava comes out of a steep-sided hole called a crater.

Volcanoes can be grouped by their shape. Stratovolcanoes are cone-shaped with steep slopes. They explode often because their thick lava traps gas underneath. Shield volcanoes have gentle slopes and are made almost completely of lava. They may be very large and have several vents. Their thin, smooth lava flows quickly.

Mountains

Mountains form where tectonic plates crash into each other. There are three main kinds of mountains: fold mountains, fault-block mountains, and volcanic mountains.

Fold mountains form from colliding plates. Layers of sedimentary rock fold upward as they are squeezed. Fault-block mountains form from movement along large faults. Large blocks of rock drop down, leaving other places high. Volcanic mountains form when magma below Earth's surface pushes rock layers upward, forming domes.

© Houghton Mifflin Harcourt Publishing Company
Core Skills Science, G6 SV 9781419098468

Name _____ Date _____

What Changes Do Moving Plates Cause?

Fill in the blanks in the diagram below.

Web Diagram

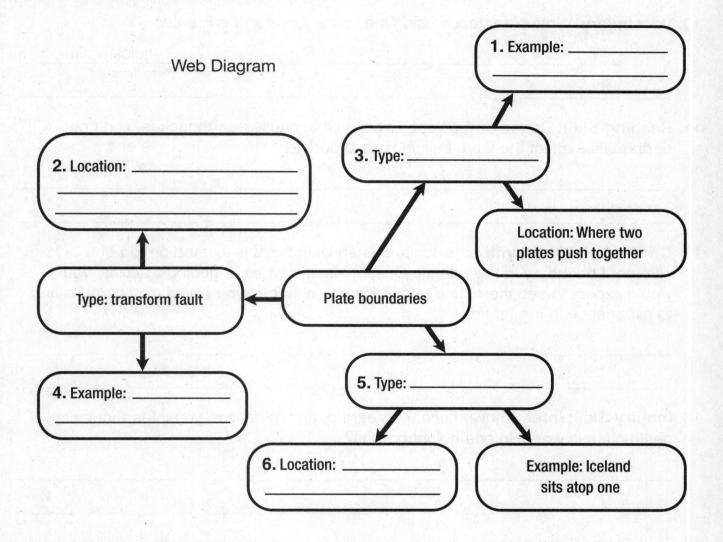

Fill in the blanks.

7. During an earthquake, the point on the surface directly above the focus is the

_____.

8. Volcanoes form when _____ is pushed through Earth's crust.

Earth Science
Core Skills Science, G6 SV 9781419098468

9. Main Idea What geologic events are likely to take place at convergent plate boundaries?

_____

_____

10. Vocabulary Write a sentence using the terms *focus* and *epicenter*.

_____

_____

11. Reading Skill: Cause and Effect Explain what causes earthquakes, and how earthquakes affect the land, buildings, and people.

_____

_____

12. Critical Thinking: Synthesis Iceland is an island that is located on top of a divergent boundary in the Atlantic Ocean. List the types of geologic activity you would expect to see there, and suggest some changes you would expect the island to experience in the future.

_____

_____

13. Inquiry Skill: Infer A town suffers an earthquake. What can you infer about why destruction is worse in one neighborhood?

_____

_____

14. Test Prep Which of these geologic features would you expect to find at a transform fault boundary?

A active volcanoes

B a mountain chain

C faults

D hydrothermal vents

Why Are Fossil Fuels Limited?

Formation and Use of Fossil Fuels

The main fossil fuels are coal, petroleum or oil, and natural gas. Most coal formed from the remains of plants that lived during the Carboniferous period. The Carboniferous period was a time in Earth's history that lasted from 360 million to 286 million years ago. During that period, Earth's climate was warm and the land was covered with swamps and shallow seas. Huge ferns and trees grew in the swamps. Green algae, a plant-like living thing, covered the seas.

When the plants and animals died, they were buried under sediments. Over time, upper layers pressed down on the remains and squeezed them together. This pressure forced out the water and left behind substances rich in carbon and hydrogen. The plant and animal remains slowly turned into coal, oil, or natural gas. Oil and natural gas were formed from remains of plants and animals buried on the ocean floor.

Coal was formed in swamps. Dead plant material built up, forming peat. As peat was buried under soil, water was forced out. Over many years, pressure squeezed the material into "soft" coal. This is the most widely used coal. Higher temperatures and pressure on the coal layer formed "hard" coal. This is almost pure carbon.

Sources of Energy

Fossil fuels are a part of an energy chain that begins with the Sun. Energy from the Sun is stored in fossil fuels. Burning the fuels releases the stored energy.

One way fossil fuels provide energy is by making electricity. Many electric power plants burn coal. Heat from burning the coal is used to boil water. Steam from the boiling water turns turbines, which are like large fans. Machines called generators change the energy of the spinning turbines to electric energy.

Coal-burning Power Plant

Fossil fuels may not be the best choice for providing energy. One problem is that fossil fuels are a nonrenewable resource. This means they cannot be replaced quickly or easily. People are using fossil fuels much more quickly than natural processes can replace them. At these rates, Earth will run out of fossil fuels someday.

Burning fossil fuels also pollutes, or dirties, the air and water. In the past, smoke and soot produced by burning coal filled the air and almost blocked out the Sun. People died from lung illnesses caused by the pollution. Today, laws and better ways of using fossil fuels help prevent pollution. However, air pollution from factories and automobiles is still a problem.

Conservation of Fossil Fuels

Because we are running out of fossil fuels quickly, scientists are learning how to make cleaner, renewable sources of energy to replace them. Some of these new energy sources, such as solar power, are available today. Solar power comes from the Sun, a renewable resource. Renewable resources can be used day after day without running out.

Tips for Saving Energy

Save energy by turning off lights, televisions, and electric items when not in use. Recycle materials such as paper, plastic, and metal. Change clothes to fit the weather, so you use the smallest amount of heat or air conditioning. Tightly close windows and doors to keep warm or cool air inside the house.

Make your home energy efficient. Insulate the attic, outside and basement walls, ceilings, floors, and crawl spaces in your home. Repair holes or cracks around your walls, ceilings, windows, doors, light and plumbing fixtures, switches, and electrical outlets to prevent air leaking into or out of your home. Close fireplace dampers when not in use. Make sure your appliances and heating and cooling systems are properly maintained. Replace standard (incandescent) light bulbs and fixtures with compact or standard fluorescent lamps.

Name _____   Date _____

Why Are Fossil Fuels Limited?

Write answers to the questions on the lines below.

1. What are the main fossil fuels?

_____

2. What is at the beginning of the energy chain that ends with fossil fuels?

_____

3. Why are fossil fuels a nonrenewable resource?

_____

4. What are some ways to conserve energy?

_____

_____

Put the following steps of coal formation in the correct sequence.
Write 1, 2, 3, and 4.

5. ____   High temperatures and pressure form "hard" coal.

____   Water is squeezed out of plant material in peat.

____   Pressure squeezes material into "soft" coal.

____   Dead plant materials in swamps form peat.

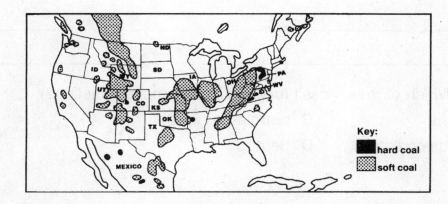

Earth Science
Core Skills Science, G6 SV 9781419098468

6. Main Idea Describe fossil fuel formation. Where are the fuels found?

_____

_____

7. Vocabulary Write a paragraph using the terms *nonrenewable resource* and *fossil fuels*. Explain why fossil fuels should be used wisely.

_____

_____

_____

8. Reading Skill: Problem-Solution What are two ways people have begun to solve the problem of pollution?

_____

_____

9. Critical Thinking: Evaluation What are some advantages and disadvantages of burning fossil fuels for their energy? Why are scientists researching new energy sources?

_____

_____

_____

10. Inquiry Skill: Use Models How would you make a model showing how coal is formed, using common materials?

_____

_____

11. Test Prep Which of these fossil fuels is used to make gasoline?

   A natural gas   **C** petroleum

   B bituminous coal   **D** peat

How Can Renewable Energy Be Used?

The Importance of Renewable Resources

Fossil fuels are nonrenewable, and we are running out of them. However, people will always need energy. Therefore, people are thinking of ways to use renewable resources. These resources include solar energy, wind, biomass, and fuel cells.

We must find and develop renewable sources of energy for the future. Renewable resources, such as the Sun, wind, and moving water, can be used day after day without running out. Renewable resources do not run out or pollute the air like fossil fuels.

Solar Energy

Energy from the Sun is called solar energy. It is a renewable resource. People use solar collectors on their houses to make energy. Photovoltaic, or PV, cells collect sunlight and change it directly into electricity. PV cells can even be used to power spacecraft.

Wind Energy

Wind power is a growing source of energy that uses wind turbines with spinning blades. A generator changes the energy of the spinning turbine into electrical energy. The amount of energy depends on the size of the turbine and the wind speed. Today's wind turbines may be as tall as a 20-story building and have three blades that measure 60 meters or more across. Wind turbines work best in areas where steady winds blow most of the time.

Fields with dozens of wind turbines are called wind farms. The turbines work together to make large amounts of electricity.

The three largest wind farms in California make enough electricity to power a city the size of San Francisco. Some countries use wind power to generate 10 percent or more of their electricity.

Energy from Moving Water

Electric energy made from moving water is called hydroelectric energy. Most hydroelectric power plants are built near a dam. Water runs through tunnels to turbines, making them spin. The energy from the spinning turbines is changed into electricity.

Nuclear Energy

Nuclear energy is created from the metal uranium. Uranium is made of tiny particles called atoms. The center of an atom is the nucleus. The nucleus of a uranium atom can be split into pieces. This process is called nuclear fission, and it releases large amounts of energy. Harnessing this energy creates nuclear power. Nuclear power plants do not pollute the air, but they create deadly waste materials that are difficult to dispose of.

Geothermal Energy

Heat energy from inside Earth is called geothermal energy. When magma inside the Earth heats underground pools of water, hot springs or geysers are formed. The heated water can be used to heat homes and to make electricity.

Biomass

Each year, many tons of once-living matter, or biomass, goes to waste. Biomass includes unused plant parts from farms, food scraps, and animal wastes. Biomass can be burned in a power plant to make electricity.

Biomass is also used to make biofuels. Ethanol is made from unwanted corn products and is burned as fuel. Burning biomass creates much less air pollution than fossil fuels.

Alternative Fuels for Vehicles

Alternative fuels are fuels other than those made from petroleum. Making and using alternative fuels for vehicles is a key to conserving petroleum products, or gas and oil.

One kind of alternative fuel is biodiesel. Scientists are working on engines that run on ethanol only. Even vegetable oils can be used to run car engines.

Vehicles can also run on electricity. Today, subway trains and many buses run on electricity. Hybrid electric cars, or cars that use two different forms of fuel, use both a small gasoline engine and an electric motor that runs on batteries.

Many carmakers are working on cars that run on hydrogen fuel cells. In a hydrogen fuel cell, a gas called hydrogen joins with oxygen from the air. This reaction makes a lot of energy, and the only waste is water.

How Can Renewable Energy Be Used?

Match each definition to its term.

Definitions

____ **1.** an energy source that will not run out

____ **2.** energy from the Sun

____ **3.** a device that converts light directly into electricity

____ **4.** energy produced from moving water

____ **5.** thermal energy from the Earth's interior

____ **6.** once-living matter

____ **7.** energy from nuclear fisson

Terms

a. biomass

b. hydroelectric energy

c. geothermal energy

d. solar energy

e. renewable resource

f. photovoltaic cell

g. nuclear energy

Fill in the blanks. Use the pie chart to answer questions 8 and 9.

Renewable Energy Sources in the United States

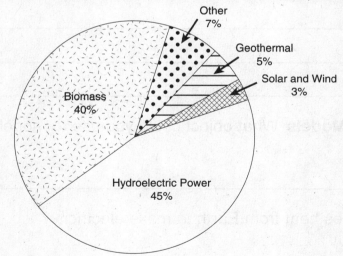

8. The largest source of renewable energy in the U.S. is _____.

9. The smallest amount of renewable energy used in the U.S. comes from

_____.

10. Each year, many tons of once-living matter, or _____, go to waste.

11. Main Idea Describe some ways that renewable energy resources can be used to power automobiles.

_____

_____

_____

12. Vocabulary Define the term *hydroelectric energy*. Describe how this kind of energy is made.

_____

_____

_____

13. Reading Skill: Main Idea and Details What is biomass, and why is it a renewable energy resource?

_____

_____

_____

14. Critical Thinking: Evaluation What would you say to someone who said that the United States should switch from fossil fuels to nuclear energy?

_____

_____

_____

_____

15. Inquiry Skill: Use Models What object could you use to model the effects of wind on a wind turbine?

_____

_____

16. Test Prep What uses heat from Earth to make electricity?

   A solar cells

   B hydroelectric dams

   C geothermal plants

   D hydrogen fuel cells

Why Does Weather Occur?

Composition of the Atmosphere

The atmosphere is the mixture of gases, liquids, and solids that surrounds Earth. Earth's atmosphere is divided into different layers. About 90 percent of Earth's atmosphere is in the lowest layer, the troposphere. Most of Earth's weather occurs in the troposphere, including clouds and rain.

The stratosphere, the layer above the troposphere, is where ozone gas is found. Ozone is important. It absorbs harmful rays from the Sun. The mesosphere is the layer above the stratosphere. It is the coldest layer of the atmosphere. The thermosphere is the layer above the mesosphere through which the space shuttle sometimes travels. The top layer of the atmosphere is called the exosphere. The exosphere has no outside edge. It just blends into outer space.

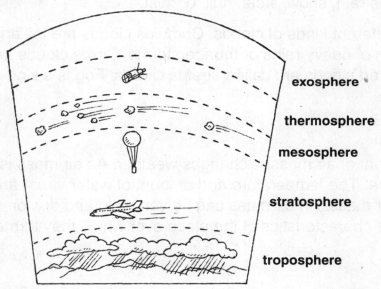

exosphere

thermosphere

mesosphere

stratosphere

troposphere

Energy from the Sun

The Sun gives off a huge amount of energy. Earth gets only a small part of that energy, but this small amount causes Earth's weather. About 30 percent of the Sun's energy that reaches Earth is reflected back into space. Earth's atmosphere absorbs about 19 percent. Earth's surface absorbs 51 percent of the energy.

The atmosphere is heated by convection, the transfer of heat by a gas or liquid. Earth's surface is heated by the Sun. Then the surface sends heat into the atmosphere.

Air rises or sinks because of differences in density. Warm air is less dense than cold air, so warm air rises. Cold air is more dense than warm air, so cold air sinks. The movement of warm air and cold air creates a loop called a convection current. This current may form in air or water.

Warm air and cold air also create differences in air pressure. As warm air rises, the air pressure below it gets lower. Think of the warm air as pressing down on the cooler air below. When the warm air rises, it stops pressing down. This lowers the air pressure. As it sinks, cold air presses down on air below it. This raises air pressure.

Cloud Formation

The Sun's energy powers Earth's water cycle. The Sun's energy causes liquid water to evaporate, or change from a liquid into a gas. Liquid water becomes water vapor, which moves though Earth's atmosphere.

Water vapor can change back to liquid water. It can also change into a solid. The solid form of water vapor is ice. These changes are called condensation. Water vapor can condense and form tiny water drops. Clouds are made up of millions of water drops. Sometimes the water drops in clouds fall to Earth's surface. This is called precipitation and may occur as rain, snow, sleet, hail, or mist.

There are different kinds of clouds. Cumulus clouds are tall and puffy. Cumulonimbus clouds are a sign of heavy rains or thunderstorms. Cirrus clouds are high above the Earth. Low, layered clouds are called stratus clouds. Fog is a kind of cloud that touches the ground.

Air Masses

The movement of air masses changes weather. An air mass is a body of air that can cover a large area. The temperature and amount of water vapor are about the same throughout an air mass. An air mass can be very cold and dry, or warm and wet. Air masses have the characteristics of the place over which they formed.

Fronts

A front is the place where two air masses meet along a boundary. Air masses on either side of the boundary often have different temperatures and air pressures. These differences often cause precipitation.

Fronts are named for the type of air mass that is moving into an area. A cold front can bring storms, followed by cool, dry weather. A warm front often brings light, steady precipitation and warmer weather.

Name _____ Date _____

Why Does Weather Occur?

Fill in the blanks.

1. About 27 percent of the Sun's energy is _____ by clouds and the atmosphere back into space.

2. The Earth's atmosphere _____ about 19 percent of the Sun's energy.

3. Earth's _____ absorbs about 51 percent of the Sun's energy, which heats the atmosphere.

Write answers to the questions on the lines below.

4. Why does cold air sink?

_____

5. What is a loop of moving air that forms in both air and water?

_____

6. What is precipitation?

_____

_____

7. How do air masses get their characteristics?

_____

8. What is a front?

_____

9. Main Idea What is an air mass?

_____

_____

10. Vocabulary Write a short paragraph using the terms *air mass*, *front*, and *precipitation*.

_____

_____

_____

11. Reading Skill: Compare and Contrast How do cumulus clouds and stratus clouds compare?

_____

_____

12. Critical Thinking: Synthesis What would you conclude about the weather if the barometric pressure was dropping and you could see cumulonimbus clouds in the sky?

_____

_____

13. Inquiry Skill: Record Data Make a chart on a separate sheet of paper to record these data: the boiling point of water on a flat ocean beach is 100°C (212°F). The boiling point of water on a mountain 1,500 m above sea level is 95°C (203°F). What is the boiling point of water at 3,000 m above sea level?

14. Test Prep In which layer of the atmosphere does most weather occur?

   A troposphere

   B stratosphere

   C mesosphere

   D exosphere

How Can Storms Be Tracked?

Meteorology

Meteorology is the study of weather. Meteorologists are people who study weather. They collect a lot of information and use it to explain and predict the weather. They compare the information they collect with pictures taken by satellites. They also use computers to help them find patterns in the weather.

Meteorologists use different instruments to study weather. Thermometers measure temperature. Rain gauges measure rainfall. Other instruments measure air pressure, wind speed, and humidity. Meteorologists may also use weather balloons to carry instruments into the atmosphere. The instruments collect information about the weather.

Meteorologists use weather satellites to measure the temperature in clouds. Satellites also measure how dense clouds are and how much water vapor the clouds have. Satellites can measure tiny amounts of dust or ash that may be in clouds. All this information helps meteorologists understand how the weather changes under different conditions.

Radar helps meteorologists understand the weather. Doppler radar picks up images of storms. It can give the direction a storm is moving. This information helps meteorologists know in advance if a thunderstorm or a tornado will hit a certain place.

All of these tools help meteorologists track and predict the weather. Weather forecasting today is better than ever before. However, Earth's atmosphere is very complicated. No one can be completely certain about tomorrow's weather.

Dangerous Weather

An air mass is a large body of air with the same temperature and amount of water vapor throughout. Air masses bump into each other at a front. A front may be a cold front, a warm front, or a stationary front. Some fronts cause strong storms.

A thunderstorm is a small but very strong weather system with heavy rain and strong winds. A thunderstorm forms at a front where warm, wet air rises above cooler air. Cumulus clouds form first. If the cloud has a lot of water vapor, it becomes a cumulonimbus cloud. If the air stays unstable, thunderstorms will continue to form.

Thunderstorms produce thunder and lightning. Lightning occurs when opposite electrical charges build up inside a thundercloud or between a cloud and the ground. Lightning heats air around the flash. This causes the air to expand and contract very quickly. Thunder is the sound make by this quick movement of air.

In winter, fronts may bring ice storms or blizzards. Blizzards are snowstorms with high winds. They form in the same way as rainstorms, but they do not have thunder and lightning.

Hurricanes

Hurricanes, large rotating storms that form over the ocean, are the strongest storms on Earth. They may be 100 miles to 930 miles in diameter! They have constant winds of at least 74 mph.

A hurricane begins as a low-pressure system over warm ocean water. Thunderstorms form and begin to rotate around the low-pressure area. Water vapor from the ocean water fuels the storm. As the storm gets stronger, the pressure in the center, or eye, of the storm gets lower.

The hurricane grows over the warm ocean. If it moves over cooler water, it loses power. If it moves over land, it is no longer fed by water vapor. The storm quickly loses energy and slows down. However, strong winds and rain can cause extreme damage on land.

Tornadoes

Hurricanes are the most powerful storms. But tornadoes can be the most violent. A tornado is a violently rotating column of air that can form during a thunderstorm. The top of the column is connected to a thunderstorm cloud. The bottom of the column touches the ground.

Tornadoes are shaped like funnels, or cones. The winds in the cone rotate so fast that they pull objects apart. Tornadoes can cause great damage, but their path is narrow.

Name _____ Date _____

How Can Storms Be Tracked?

Fill in the blanks.

1. _____ radar picks up images of storms and determines the direction they are moving.

2. In the first diagram below, cumulus clouds form as warm, moist air is pushed upward at a(n) _____.

How thunderstorms develop

3. In the second diagram, the cumulus cloud has sufficient moisture and develops into a(n) _____ cloud.

4. In the third diagram, thunderstorms continue to develop at the front as long as plenty of moisture makes the air _____.

5. _____ heats the air around the flash and causes it to expand and contract rapidly.

6. Snowstorms called _____ have high winds but usually do not have thunder and lightning.

7. A(n) _____ begins as thunderstorms begin to rotate around a low-pressure zone over warm tropical waters.

8. _____ are funnel-shaped clouds with rapidly rotating winds.

9. Main Idea How do fronts cause thunderstorms to develop?

_____

_____

10. Vocabulary Write a sentence using the terms *thunderstorm* and *tornado*.

_____

_____

11. Reading Skill: Text Structure What are the steps in the development of a hurricane?

_____

_____

_____

12. Critical Thinking: Analyze Why are hurricanes referred to as powerful, while tornadoes are referred to as violent?

_____

_____

13. Inquiry Skill: Predict What will happen to a hurricane as it begins to move onto land?

_____

_____

14. Test Prep A severe storm that forms quickly and has heavy rain and lightning is called a

A hurricane.

B thunderstorm.

C tornado.

D blizzard.

How Does the Sun Affect Earth?

The Sun

The Sun is a huge ball of hot, glowing gas. More than 1 million Earths could fit inside the Sun! The Sun is about 150,000,000 km (93,000,000 mi) away from Earth. It is the star closest to Earth. Life on Earth depends on the Sun, which is the main source of Earth's energy.

The Sun's gravity keeps Earth and the other planets in orbit around the Sun. The Sun is very hot. A hot day on Earth may be 100°F (38°C). Inside the Sun, the temperature is about 15,000,000°C. That is hot!

Inside the Sun, hydrogen is changed into helium. This change occurs through a process called nuclear fusion. Nuclear fusion gives off huge amounts of energy.

Day and Night

Life on Earth depends on the Sun, which is the main source of energy for Earth. Plants need sunlight to grow. Plants use the energy in sunlight to make their own food through photosynthesis. In turn, plants are food for other living things.

From Earth, the Sun seems to move across the sky. It rises each morning in the east and sets in the west each evening. The Sun seems to move because Earth rotates, just like a top spins. Earth spins on its axis, which is an imaginary line that runs through the center of Earth.

Earth's axis passes through the North Pole and the South Pole. Each complete turn of Earth on its axis is called a full rotation. A full rotation takes one day, or 24 hours. As Earth rotates, one half of the planet faces the Sun, so that side has daytime. One half of the planet faces away from the Sun, where it is nighttime.

The Year and the Seasons

Earth moves around the Sun. This movement is called its orbit. A complete orbit around the Sun is called a revolution. Earth orbits the Sun in about 365 days, or one year.

Earth's axis is tilted, so sometimes the North Pole points toward the Sun. At other times, the North Pole points away from the Sun. This causes seasons.

In most places, the weather changes with the seasons. We live in the Northern Hemisphere, which is tilted toward the Sun in the summer. The Sun's rays hit the ground more directly, so the weather is warm.

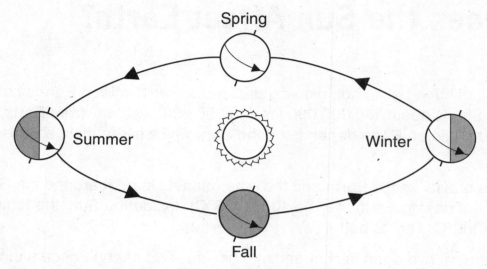

Earth's Seasons

In winter, the Northern Hemisphere is tilted away from the Sun. The Sun is low in the sky, and days are shorter. The Sun's rays hit the ground at an angle. This makes the winter days cool. When the Northern Hemisphere is tilted toward the Sun, the Southern Hemisphere is tilted away. So its seasons are opposite.

The beginnings of seasons are marked by dates called equinoxes and solstices. These dates are based on Earth's orbit around the Sun. Equinoxes are the dates when spring and fall begin. Solstices are dates when summer and winter begin.

During an equinox, the length of day and night is almost equal everywhere on Earth. The days get longer until the summer solstice, the longest day of the year. Then the days get shorter until the fall equinox, when the day and night are equal again. The days continue to get shorter until the winter solstice, the shortest day of the year.

Near the equator, days last about 12 hours all year long. The farther from the equator a place is, the longer summer days are. At the North Pole, the Sun may shine all day and all night in summer.

Constellations

Long ago, people saw shapes or pictures in groups of stars. These groups are called constellations. Asterisms are groups of stars that are parts of constellations. The Big Dipper and Little Dipper are asterisms. They are part of the constellations Ursa Major and Ursa Minor. There are some constellations that can only be seen from the Northern Hemisphere and some that can be seen only from the Southern Hemisphere.

How Does the Sun Affect Earth?

Fill in the blanks.

1. The Sun is the closest _____ to Earth.

2. The Sun is essential to life on Earth and is the ultimate source of

_____ for Earth.

3. As Earth _____, the half facing the Sun has day, while the other
half has night.

4. Earth takes one year to complete one _____, or orbit, around
the Sun.

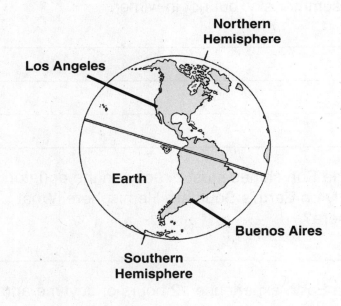
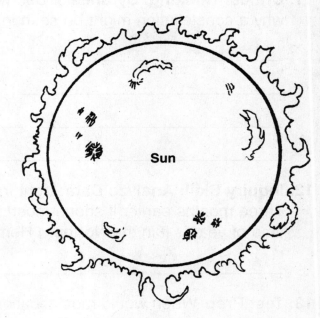

5. In the diagram above, it is summer in the city of _____.

6. It is winter in Buenos Aires when the _____ Hemisphere is tilted
toward the Sun.

7. Asterisms are star groupings that form parts of patterns or groupings of stars called

_____.

8. Main Idea Explain why Earth has seasons.

_____

_____

9. Vocabulary What is the difference between Earth's rotation and Earth's revolution?

_____

_____

10. Reading Skill: Text Structure List four ways the Sun affects Earth.

_____

_____

11. Critical Thinking: Synthesis Use what you know about Earth's revolution to explain why a constellation might be seen in the summer sky, but not in winter.

_____

_____

_____

_____

12. Inquiry Skill: Analyze Data Light from the Sun shines most directly on the equator. Three months earlier it shone most directly on Earth's Southern Hemisphere. What time of year is it in the Northern Hemisphere?

_____

13. Test Prep When would most locations on Earth experience 12 hours of daytime and 12 hours of nighttime?

  A summer solstice

  B fall equinox

  C December

  D May

How Do Eclipses Occur?

Phases of the Moon

The Moon is a satellite of Earth. A satellite is an object that orbits a planet. Scientists have made satellites that orbit Earth.

The Moon is Earth's natural satellite. Earth's gravity keeps the Moon in its orbit around Earth. Together, Earth and its Moon orbit the Sun.

The Moon does not give off its own light. Instead, the Moon reflects the light of the Sun. The Sun lights the half of the Moon that is facing it. As the Moon orbits Earth, different parts of the Moon's near side are lit by the Sun. That is why the Moon's shape seems to change from night to night. Each different shape of the Moon is called a phase of the Moon. Phases change in a cycle that repeats about once a month.

New Moon   **Full Moon**   **Last Quarter**

The Moon

Temperature (at the equator)	Noon: 127°C (260°F) Night: -173°C (-279°F)
Rotation	27 days, 7 hours, 43 minutes
Revolution (time to orbit around Earth)	27 days, 7 hours, 43 minutes

Lunar Eclipse

When an object blocks a path of light, a shadow forms. Earth's shadow has two parts. The umbra is the darkest part of the shadow. The penumbra is the lighter part. It surrounds the umbra.

A lunar eclipse occurs when the Moon passes through Earth's shadow. Earth is between the Sun and the Moon and blocks the Sun's light from reaching the Moon's surface.

There are three types of lunar eclipse. A total lunar eclipse occurs when the whole Moon passes through the umbra. A partial lunar eclipse occurs when part of the Moon passes through the umbra. A penumbral eclipse occurs when the Moon passes only through the penumbra.

Solar Eclipse

Sometimes the Moon blocks the Sun's light and casts a shadow. The Moon's shadow also has an umbra and a penumbra.

A solar eclipse occurs when the Moon passes between Earth and the Sun. The Moon blocks the path of the Sun's light and casts a shadow on Earth. In a full or partial solar eclipse, the Moon's shadow covers only a small part of Earth's surface.

During a total solar eclipse, the sky gets dark as the Moon moves in front of the Sun. The corona is a shining ring of light from the Sun's outside edge. It is all you can see of the Sun during a total eclipse.

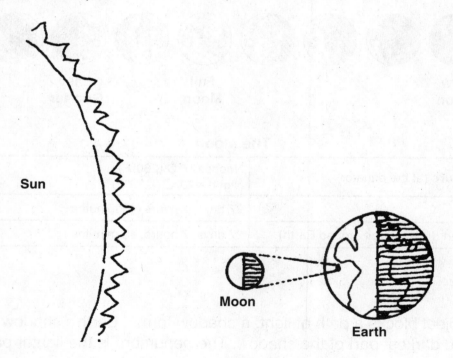

Sun

Moon

Earth

Planetary Transits

Sometimes a planet passes between the Sun and Earth. This is called planetary transit. From Earth, only Venus and Mercury have planetary transits because they are the only two planets between Earth and the Sun.

Planetary transits occur much less often than eclipses. Why? It takes much longer for a planet to orbit the Sun than it does for the Moon to orbit Earth.

How Do Eclipses Occur?

Write answers to the questions on the lines below.

1. Why does the Moon appear to change shape from night to night?

_____

_____

2. What are the two regions of Earth's shadow during an eclipse?

_____

3. What part of the Sun is visible during a total solar eclipse?

_____

4. What is planetary transit?

_____

_____

5. From Earth, what two planets have planetary transits?

_____

6. Main Idea Explain the difference between a solar eclipse and a lunar eclipse.

_____

_____

_____

_____

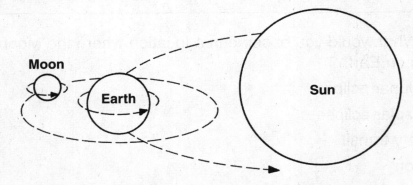

7. Vocabulary Define the terms *umbra* and *penumbra*.

_____

_____

_____

8. Reading Skill: Sequence The word *wane* means "to decrease gradually in power or intensity." Sketch and label several waning moon phases starting with a full Moon.

9. Critical Thinking: Analyze Explain why you won't see the Moon at night during its new moon phase.

_____

_____

_____

10. Inquiry Skill: Infer A transit of a certain planet is never visible from Earth. What can you infer about the orbit of that planet around the Sun?

_____

_____

11. Test Prep What would you observe in a location where the Moon's penumbral shadow falls on Earth?

A a partial lunar eclipse

B a partial solar eclipse

C a planetary transit

D a full moon

What Causes Tides?

Tides

At low tide, a beach may be very wide. Six hours later, the beach may be very narrow. At high tide, ocean waves may cover the beach.

A tide is a daily change in the level of the ocean along a coast. Every seashore in the world is affected by tides. Tides are caused mainly by the Moon's gravity. The Moon is much smaller than Earth. But it still has gravity that pulls on Earth's oceans. The pull of the Moon's gravity, with the pull of the Sun's gravity, causes tides to rise and fall.

Tides cause the ocean to stick out, or bulge, on the sides of Earth facing toward and away from the Moon. Each is called a tidal bulge. As Earth rotates, different parts of its surface are under tidal bulges. The pull of the Moon's gravity is strongest on a tidal bulge that is facing the Moon. The pull is weakest on the side of Earth farthest away from the Moon.

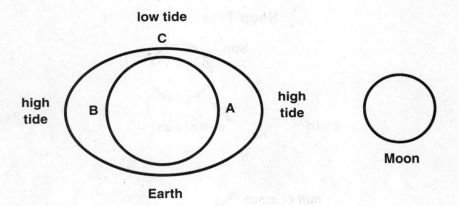

Most ocean shores have two high tides and two low tides. Two times each day, the water along the shore rises. Two times each day, the water falls. During ebb tides, the water level drops from high to low. During flood tides, the water level rises from low to high. The times of high tides and low tides are different each day.

The cycle of tides changes in other ways, too. Sometimes the Sun, the Moon, and Earth are all in a line. When this happens, the Sun and the Moon pull on Earth in the same direction. This causes a spring tide. Spring tides usually have higher high tides and lower low tides than normal. Spring tides happen during the full moon and new moon phases.

Spring Tide

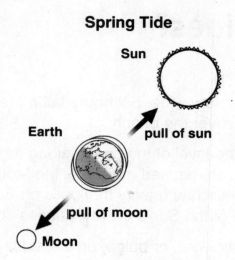

Sometimes the Moon and the Sun pull on Earth from different directions. When the Sun and the Moon are at right angles to Earth, tidal bulges become smaller. This causes a neap tide. Neap tides occur during the first quarter and third quarter phases of the Moon.

Neap Tide

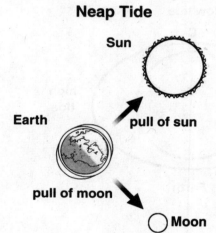

Tracking the Tides

The tidal range is the difference between the water level at high tide and the water level at low tide. The shape of the land and the depth of the water affect a place's tidal range.

The Bay of Fundy, in Canada, has the greatest tidal range on Earth. The bay is shaped like a funnel. This shape gives the Bay of Fundy its tidal range of 50 feet. Each day, the water level at high tide is 50 feet higher than the water level at low tide.

Other places have lower tidal ranges. Grand Isle, Louisiana, has a tidal range of only 1 foot. It has only one high tide and one low tide each day. People who live or work near the coast must be aware of the tide cycle. Tide charts tell them when high tides and low tides will occur.

What Causes Tides?

Write answers to the questions on the lines below.

1. What are the bulges of the oceans at the sides of Earth facing toward and away from the Moon called?

   _____

2. How often do most ocean shorelines experience two high tides and two low tides?

   _____

3. What tides are produced when the Sun, the Moon, and Earth are all in a line?

   _____

4. What tides are produced when the Sun and the Moon are at right angles to each other relative to Earth?

   _____

5. What is the difference in the water level between high tide and low tide called?

   _____

6. What two things affect a location's tidal range?

   _____

7. **Main Idea** What are tides and how are they caused?

   _____

   _____

8. Vocabulary Write a paragraph using the terms *tidal range*, *spring tides*, and *neap tides*.

_____

_____

_____

_____

9. Reading Skill: Cause and Effect An area experiences extra-high tides and extra-low tides. What causes this?

_____

_____

10. Critical Thinking: Apply The Moon's mass is about 1.2 percent of Earth's mass. If the Moon were less massive, what would the effect be on Earth's tidal bulges?

_____

_____

_____

11. Inquiry Skill: Compare Is the difference between high and low tides greater for spring tides or neap tides? Explain.

_____

_____

_____

12. Test Prep Tides that are receding from high tide to low tide are

A ebb tides.

B flood tides.

C spring tides.

D neap tides.

What Are Building Blocks of Matter?

Atoms

An atom is the smallest unit of an element. It is the basic building block of matter. The nucleus is the central part of the atom. It contains positively charged particles called protons and uncharged particles called neutrons. Negatively charged moving particles called electrons surround the nucleus.

In 1911, British scientist Earnest Rutherford developed a nuclear model that states an atom consists of a positive nucleus surrounded by negative electrons. Today's model of the atom describes electrons as moving in cloud-like regions called orbitals.

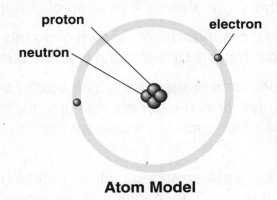

Atom Model

Ions and Isotopes

The atomic number is the number of protons in an atom. An oxygen atom has 8 protons in its nucleus; its atomic number is 8. Neutral atoms have the same number of electrons and protons.

An ion is an atom that has more or fewer electrons than protons. Positive ions have more protons than electrons. A sodium ion with 11 protons and 10 electrons has a net charge of +1. Negative ions have more electrons than protons.

Isotopes are atoms with the same number of protons and a different number of neutrons. Except for isotopes of hydrogen, isotopes are named for the number of particles in the nucleus. For example, the isotope carbon-14 has 14 particles: 6 protons and 8 neutrons.

Radioactivity

You can think of neutrons as the "glue" of the nucleus. Forces among the neutrons and protons keep the nucleus together. Most atoms are stable, but the nuclei of some isotopes are unstable. These isotopes are radioactive. Their nuclei become stable by giving off particles and energy, which is called radiation.

Classifying Elements

An element is a substance that cannot be broken down into other substances. All atoms of an element contain the same number of protons. Add or subtract a proton, and you have a different element.

Scientists classify elements as metals, nonmetals, and semimetals. Metals are shiny, conduct electricity and heat, and are easily shaped. Most nonmetals are dull, conduct electricity and heat poorly, and are not easily shaped. Semimetals have properties between metals and nonmetals. Semimetals conduct heat better than nonmetals.

Elements can also be described using other physical properties, such as density. Density is the mass per unit volume of a substance. A sample of an element that has a low density has less mass than the same-size sample of an element that has a high density.

In 1869, a Russian chemist organized then-known elements by mass into the first Periodic Table. Today's Periodic Table is similar to the first one but has many more elements.

Each box in the table represents one element. The box lists the element's atomic number, chemical symbol (a one- or two-letter abbreviation for the element), and name of the element. The boxes are color-coded to represent metals, nonmetals, semimetals, solids, liquids, and gases.

The elements in today's table are arranged by their atomic numbers. Hydrogen (H) has the atomic number 1, so it is first. The atomic number increases across each row from left to right. The rows are also called the periods of the table. Today's table lists more than 114 elements.

13	14	15	16	17	18
					2 **He** 4.00
5 **B** 10.81	6 **C** 12.01	7 **N** 14.01	8 **O** 16.00	9 **F** 19.00	10 **Ne** 20.18
13 **Al** 26.98	14 **Si** 28.09	15 **P** 30.97	16 **S** 32.07	17 **Cl** 35.45	18 **Ar** 39.95

Section of the Periodic Table

Elements in a Column

The Periodic Table gets its shape because of the way elements are arranged in columns, or groups. Elements in any one group have similar chemical properties. For example, the elements in the far-right column above are all gases at room temperature. The atoms of elements in a column all have similar electron arrangements.

Name _____ Date _____

What Are Building Blocks of Matter?

Fill in the blanks.

1. A(n) _____ is the smallest unit of an element.

2. An atom that has more or fewer electrons than it has protons is called a(n)

   _____.

3. Atoms with the same number of protons and different numbers of neutrons are

   called _____.

4. Isotopes with unstable nuclei are said to be _____.

5. The _____ allows you to compare the elements and understand
   their properties.

6. The number of protons in an atom is the _____.

Label the information contained in each box of an element on the Periodic Table.

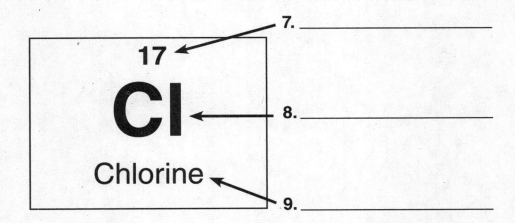

7. _____

8. _____

9. _____

10. Main Idea Where are protons, neutrons, and electrons found in an atom?

_____

_____

11. Vocabulary Write a sentence using the terms *electron*, *ion*, and *proton*.

_____

_____

12. Reading Skill: Main Idea How did Rutherford's work help form the present-day model of the atom?

_____

_____

13. Critical Thinking: Synthesis Copper, silver, and gold are located in the same group in the periodic table. What can you infer about these elements?

_____

14. Inquiry Skill: Use Numbers Make a chart of the numbers of protons, neutrons, and electrons in an atom of each of the following elements: calcium (atomic number 20), carbon-14 (atomic number 6), lithium (atomic number 3).

15. Test Prep The elements are arranged in the Periodic Table according to what property?

   A atomic mass   **C** density

   B atomic number   **D** radioactivity

What Is Physical Change?

Physical Changes

If you add dye to water, you make a solution. The dye is the solute, and the water is the solvent. The mixture will become one solid color over time because its particles are moving. Particles of all matter are moving all the time. This motion causes particles in liquids to spread out evenly over time.

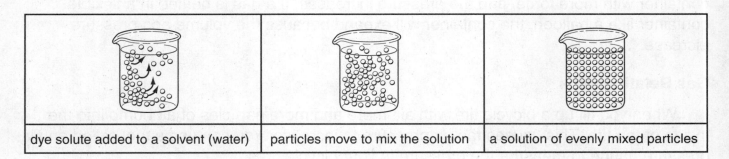

dye solute added to a solvent (water)	particles move to mix the solution	a solution of evenly mixed particles

When a solute dissolves in a solvent, a physical change takes place. During a physical change, a substance does not become a different substance. Its chemical properties stay the same.

Thermal Expansion of Solids

During physical changes that involve heating or cooling, the movement of particles changes. The energy of motion is called kinetic energy. An object's temperature tells us the average kinetic energy of its particles. When the temperature of a substance increases, the average speed of its particles also increases.

The total kinetic energy of the particles of a substance is called thermal energy. Thermal energy depends on the amount and temperature of a substance. Two samples of the same substance may have the same temperature, but the one with greater mass has more particles and more thermal energy.

When matter is heated, it expands, or gets bigger. When matter expands because of an increase in temperature, we call it thermal expansion. When the temperature increases, the particles in a solid move very quickly. They also move farther apart. This causes the whole solid to expand.

Thermal Expansion of Gases

When a substance expands, it has greater volume and takes up more space. Volume is the amount of space that a substance fills. During thermal expansion, there is an increase in volume.

Liquids have more thermal expansion than solids. Gases have the most thermal expansion. Particles of a gas move more freely than other particles. This makes gas expand to fill the whole volume of its container.

As the particles of gas move around, they bounce off each other and apply force as they hit the walls of the container. Pressure is the amount of force the particles apply within a certain area.

When temperature increases, the particles move faster. They hit the sides of their container with more force, and the pressure increases. If a gas is heated in a flexible container like a balloon, the container will expand because the volume and pressure increase.

Gas Relationships

When you fill up a bicycle tire with air, more and more particles of air bump into the inside of the tire. This causes the air pressure to increase. You can use a tool called an air pressure gauge to measure the pressure in your bicycle tires.

When you pump up a tire with an air pump, you are pushing air from the atmosphere into the tire. The air volume inside the pump decreases, but the air pressure increases. This pushes air into the tire.

The pressure, volume, and temperature of a gas work together closely. When the pressure remains the same, or constant, the volume of a gas increases as its temperature increases. When the temperature and the amount of gas are constant, the pressure of the gas increases as the volume decreases.

Temperature and State

If enough energy is added to a solid, its particles move fast enough to break the bonds that hold them together. The solid begins to melt into a liquid. The temperature, called the melting point, stays the same until all of the solid has melted. The freezing point is the temperature at which a liquid turns back into a solid.

If enough energy is added to a liquid, the particles move fast enough to change into a gas. This change is called vaporization. At the boiling point, bubbles of gas leave the liquid. The temperature stays the same until all the liquid has changed to a gas. When energy is taken away from a gas, it changes to a liquid through a process called condensation.

What Is Physical Change?

Fill in the blanks.

1. An object's temperature describes the average _____ energy of its particles.

2. The total kinetic energy of the particles of a sample is called

   _____ energy.

3. The amount of force exerted per unit area is _____.

4. If a gas is heated in a balloon, the balloon will _____ due to the increase in volume and pressure.

5. When the pressure and the amount of gas are constant, the volume increases as

   temperature _____.

6. The temperature at which a solid changes state into a liquid is called the

   _____.

7. The process that changes a liquid into a gas is _____.

8. **Main Idea** How is temperature related to the speed of particles in a substance?

   _____

   _____

   _____

9. Vocabulary Compare and contrast the terms *temperature* and *thermal energy*.

_____

_____

10. Reading Skill: Cause and Effect What happens to the volume of a gas when its temperature decreases if the pressure is held constant?

_____

_____

11. Critical Thinking: Analyze The temperature of a solid increases steadily for 3 minutes, remains 0°C for 10 minutes, and then increases again. The final sample is a liquid. What conclusion can you draw?

_____

_____

12. Inquiry Skill: Hypothesize A dozen balloons all popped when taken outside. Develop a hypothesis to explain this.

_____

_____

13. Test Prep Most substances increase in volume when temperature increases. What term describes this effect?

   A thermal expansion

   B melting point

   C freezing point

   D absolute temperature

What Is Chemical Change?

Chemical Changes

A physical change does not alter the chemical makeup of the matter being changed. However, when a chemical change takes place, a new substance is formed. In a chemical change, one group of substances changes to make new substances. For example, when the metal iron and oxygen come together in air, a chemical change occurs to form a new substance called rust.

Examples of Chemical Changes

Chemical changes take place all around you every day. A change in color is one sign of a chemical change. A chemical change causes green bananas to turn yellow as they ripen.

Some chemical changes, such as burning, happen quickly and give off large amounts of light and heat. All burning is an example of a chemical change. Burning wood in a fire, natural gas in a stove, and wax in a candle are just three examples. When gasoline in a car burns, the chemical change makes energy to make the car run. Other chemical changes take place more slowly. Many chemical changes help young animals grow into adults. Living thing cause chemical changes in the world around them, too. Moss growing on rocks makes chemicals that slowly break down the rock it grows on.

Chemical Reactions

In a compound, atoms or ions are held together by chemical bonds. These bonds are formed by electrons that the atoms or ions share. The nuclei of the atoms or ions do not change.

During chemical reactions, bonds are broken and new bonds are formed. When bonds break, energy is absorbed from the environment. When new bonds form, energy is released.

The substances that form during a chemical change usually have physical and chemical properties that are different from the first substances. The formation of one or more substances with properties and chemical compositions that differ from the original substances is called a chemical reaction. All chemical changes involve chemical reactions.

When lightning strikes, new substances form. Molecules of nitrogen gas and oxygen gas absorb energy from the lightning to form new compounds called nitrogen oxides. Nitrogen oxide molecules are made from nitrogen and oxygen atoms.

Endothermic Reactions

During an endothermic reaction, energy is absorbed. The energy that is needed to break bonds in the original substances is greater than the energy released when new bonds form. For example, the breakdown of water (H_2O) into hydrogen (H_2) and oxygen (O_2) is an endothermic reaction. A process called electrolysis can provide the energy for this reaction. During electrolysis, an electric current is sent through water.

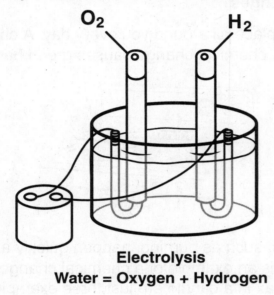

Electrolysis
Water = Oxygen + Hydrogen

Another important endothermic reaction occurs in plants. During photosynthesis, a sugar is formed from water and carbon dioxide. Plants use energy in sunlight to perform photosynthesis.

Exothermic Reactions

Exothermic reactions release energy. The energy that is needed to break the bonds in the original substances is less than the energy released when new bonds form. Exothermic reactions can give off energy as light, heat, or even sound.

In most cases, reactions with burning, flames, or an explosion are exothermic reactions. When fireworks explode, energy that is released makes loud sounds and bright lights.

Many chemical reactions that take place in your body are exothermic. One of these reactions is called respiration. In respiration, the sugar glucose ($C_6H_{12}O_6$) is broken down from food when oxygen (O_2) is present. Carbon dioxide (CO_2) and water (H_2O) are formed. The energy released during respiration helps your body work.

What Is Chemical Change?

Write answers to the questions on the lines below.

1. What happens to substances in a chemical change?

_____

_____

2. What happens to chemical bonds during a chemical change?

_____

_____

3. What reaction takes place in plants during photosynthesis?

_____

4. In what type of reaction do burning, flames, and explosions occur?

_____

5. Does the reaction that separates water (H_2O) into hydrogen (H_2) and oxygen (O_2) absorb or release energy?

_____

6. What forms of energy can exothermic reactions give off?

_____

7. Main Idea How is energy involved in a chemical change?

_____

_____

8. Vocabulary How do endothermic and exothermic reactions differ?

_____

_____

9. Reading Skill: Main Idea and Details During a chemical reaction, how do the substances that form differ from the substances that react?

_____

_____

10. Critical Thinking: Apply A chemical reaction in a lightstick causes it to give off a glowing green light. Explain why the reaction is endothermic or exothermic.

_____

_____

11. Inquiry Skill: Observe What kinds of observations can you make that might indicate a chemical change is taking place?

_____

_____

12. Test Prep Which of the following is a chemical change?

   A liquid water freezing to form ice

   B electrolysis of water to form hydrogen and oxygen

   C salt dissolving in water to form a solution

   D separation of water from a salt solution through evaporation

What Are Types of Chemical Reactions?

Classifying Reactions

In a chemical reaction, bonds in two molecules are rearranged, and the atoms form new molecules. Chemical equations describe the way atoms are grouped when substances react.

A chemical equation is a way of showing the chemical formulas and symbols of the substances that react and form in a chemical reaction. An arrow separates the "before" and "after" parts of the reaction. The substances that react are on the left side of the arrow. The substances that form are on the right side of the arrow.

Chemical Reaction Type	Generic Chemical Equation
synthesis	$A + B \longrightarrow AB$
decomposition	$AB \longrightarrow A + B$
single-replacement	$A + BC \longrightarrow B + AC$
double-replacement	$AB + CD \longrightarrow AD + CB$
combustion	Carbon compound $+ O_2 \longrightarrow CO_2 + H_2$

Chemical reactions can be grouped according to the way the atoms of the reacting substance group together or come apart. Chemical reactions can be classified as synthesis, decomposition, single-replacement, double-replacement, or combustion reactions.

Synthesis   When two substances react and form one substance, the reaction is called a synthesis reaction. Only one substance is written on the right side of the arrow in the equation.

Decomposition   In a decomposition reaction, a single substance breaks down to form two or more substances. There is only one substance on the left side of the arrow.

Single Replacement   When one element replaces another element in a compound, the reaction is called a single-replacement reaction. In the chemical equation, pure elements will be on both sides of the arrow.

Double Replacement   In a double-replacement reaction, two atoms or groups of atom switch places.

Combustion   When a carbon compound reacts with oxygen, it goes through combustion, and carbon dioxide and water are produced. Combustion is almost always an exothermic reaction.

Conservation of Matter

In any chemical reaction, the total mass of the substances does not change, even when new products form. The law of conservation of matter says that matter cannot be made or destroyed. In a chemical reaction, this means that the total mass of the substance before a chemical reaction is equal to the total mass of the substances that are produced. This is true even if you cannot see the substances that form during the reaction, such as when a gas is formed.

You can use a scale to find the mass of substances before and after a chemical reaction. For example, when fruit decays, the fruit's tissues break down, new compounds form, and gases are released. But the total mass remains the same before and after the chemical change.

Balancing Chemical Equations

Chemical equations don't just show which substances are reacting and forming in a chemical reaction. They also show the law of conservation of matter. A balanced chemical equation shows that the numbers and types of atoms are the same on both sides of the arrow.

Here is the equation for the decomposition of water: $2H_2O \rightarrow 2H_2 + O_2$. The equation is balanced because it shows there are four hydrogen atoms and two oxygen atoms on each side of the arrow. It also tells you that you need 2 molecules of water to make 2 molecules of hydrogen and 1 molecule of oxygen.

Coefficients are the numbers in front of each chemical formula. They show the amounts of each substance in the reaction.

Respiration is an exothermic reaction that gives your body the energy it needs to do the things that you do. The balanced chemical equation below shows the chemical reaction that takes place during respiration.

Glucose + Oxygen ⟶ Carbon Dioxide + Water

$$C_6H_{12}O_6 + 6O_2 \longrightarrow 6CO_2 + 6H_2O$$

What Are Types of Chemical Reactions?

Fill in the blanks.

1. A(n) _____ is a way of showing the chemical formulas and symbols of the substances that react and form in a chemical reaction.

2. The "before" and "after" parts of a chemical reaction are separated by a(n) _____ in the chemical equation.

3. In any chemical reaction, the total _____ of the substances does not change, no matter what new products form.

Fill in the blanks in the table below.

Type of Reaction	Example of Reaction
4. _____	$CaO + H_2O \rightarrow Ca(OH)_2$
5. _____	$2HgO \rightarrow 2Hg + O_2$
6. _____	$2AgNO_3 + Cu \rightarrow Cu(NO_3)_2 + 2Ag$
7. _____	$MgSO_4 + CaCl_2 \rightarrow CaSO_4 + MgCl_2$
8. _____	$CH_4 + 2O_2 \rightarrow CO_2 + 2H_2O$

9. **Main Idea** What are five types of chemical reactions?

_____

_____

_____

_____

10. Vocabulary How are balanced chemical equations related to the law of conservation of matter?

_____

_____

_____

11. Reading Skill: Classify What type of chemical reaction is represented by the following chemical equation?
$2Na + Cl_2 \longrightarrow 2NaCl$

_____

_____

12. Critical Thinking: Apply The chemical equation describing the burning of hydrogen gas is: $2H_2 + O_2 \longrightarrow 2H_2O$. Why is this both a synthesis and a combustion reaction?

_____

_____

_____

13. Inquiry Skill: Compare Compare the two sides of the following unbalanced equation. Then change the coefficient to balance the equation.
$Zn + HCl \longrightarrow ZnCl_2 + H_2$

_____

_____

_____

14. Test Prep What kind of reaction is described by the following equation?
$3CuCl_2 + 2Al \longrightarrow 2AlCl_3 + 3Cu$

A synthesis

B decomposition

C single-replacement

D double-replacement

What Is Conservation of Energy?

Energy Everywhere

Wherever you look, you see the effects of energy. Cars moving, kids playing, and water boiling all depend on some form of energy. Energy is very important to life and to our society.

What is energy? Energy and matter are basic parts of the Universe. Matter is anything that takes up space and has mass. Energy has the ability to do work. Work happens when a force moves an object in the direction of that force. Energy and work are measured using the same unit, the joule (jool).

Energy exists in many forms. Electrical energy is used in homes and workplaces. Many machines change electrical energy into the energy needed to work.

Energy changes also play important roles in nature. Plants use energy from the Sun to grow. The energy we get in our food comes from energy stored in plants or in animals that ate the plants.

Changes in energy are also important. Energy changes follow the law of conservation of energy. This law has two parts: (1) The amount of energy in a closed system always stays the same, and (2) Energy can change forms, but it cannot be created or destroyed.

In every energy transformation, some energy is lost to friction and changed to thermal or heat energy. The energy still exists. But it is not used to do work.

Potential and Kinetic Energy

Changes in energy involve potential energy and kinetic energy. Potential energy is stored energy. Kinetic energy is energy of motion. Anything that is moving has kinetic energy. Thermal energy, electricity, and sound energy also have kinetic energy.

Energy is constantly changing from potential to kinetic and back again. These back-and-forth changes can be seen in your body's motion. In your muscles, your body stores chemical potential energy from the food you eat. When you use your muscles to throw a ball, your body changes some of that chemical potential energy to mechanical kinetic energy—the energy of your moving arm.

In another example, an electric toothbrush has chemical potential energy in its battery. The potential energy changes to electrical, and then mechanical, kinetic energy.

Anything that can be bent or squeezed and then return to its natural shape, or anything that is flexible, such as a rubber band, has elastic potential energy. Think about some other common examples of energy use—a bow and arrow, a wind-up toy with a spring, a car engine powered by gasoline. Think about the forms of energy used.

Nuclear Energy

Nuclear energy, the most powerful form of energy, is released in a nuclear reaction. In this reaction, nuclei of atoms of one element are changed into nuclei of atoms of a different element.

Nuclear reactions occur in nature. The Sun and other stars are powered by a nuclear reaction called fusion. In a fusion reaction, small nuclei join together for form new nuclei. Extreme temperatures and pressures in the cores of stars enable fusion reactions. Large amounts of energy are released in this process.

Nuclear power plants use another type of nuclear reaction called fission. Fission involves splitting nuclei of the elements uranium or plutonium to release energy. The heat that results from fission in a nuclear power plant is used to turn water into steam, which is then used to make electricity.

Nuclei are made up of protons and neutrons. But the mass of a nucleus is less than the sum of the masses of its protons and neutrons. This difference in mass represents the energy that holds the nucleus together. In a nuclear reaction, this energy is released.

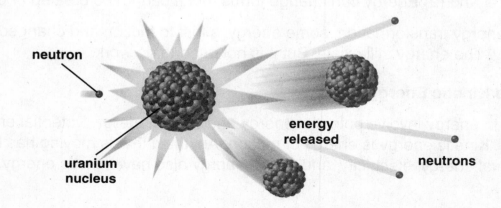

neutron

uranium nucleus

energy released

neutrons

Name _____ Date _____

What Is Conservation of Energy?

Fill in the blanks.

1. The second part of the law of conservation of energy is that energy can change forms, but it cannot be _____.

2. Moving objects, thermal energy, electricity, and sound energy have _____ energy.

3. Chemical compounds, an object lifted up, a rubber band, and your muscles have _____ energy.

4. When nuclei of atoms of one element are changed into nuclei of atoms of a different element, _____ energy is released.

Fill in the blanks in the table below.

Example	Energy Transformation
5. A rubber band in a toy airplane unwinds.	Elastic potential energy changes to mechanical _____ energy.
6. You throw a ball.	_____ potential energy changes to mechanical kinetic energy.
7. You flip the switch of an electric toothbrush.	Chemical potential energy in the battery changes to electrical _____ energy, which changes to mechanical kinetic energy.

8. Main Idea Describe some properties of energy.

_____

_____

9. Vocabulary Explain the difference between potential energy and kinetic energy. Give an example of how one can be transformed into the other.

_____

_____

_____

10. Reading Skill: Draw Conclusions Describe how Earth would be affected if it no longer got energy from the Sun.

_____

_____

11. Critical Thinking: Analyze A kitchen blender transforms electrical energy into mechanical energy. Why is the amount of mechanical energy produced less than the amount of electrical energy used?

_____

_____

12. Inquiry Skill: Compare Nuclear fusion and nuclear fission both release huge amounts of energy. How are the two processes different?

_____

_____

13. Test Prep Which of the following can be described as kinetic energy?

A chemical energy

B gravitational energy

C elastic energy

D mechanical energy

How Do Waves Transfer Energy?

Types of Waves

Have you ever watched ripples spread across a pond or huge waves roll across the surface of the ocean? If so, you have seen waves. A wave is a disturbance that carries energy, but not matter, from one place to another. When a wave travels through water, the water molecules are briefly moved from their rest positions. The disturbance that caused the wave is passed on from one molecule to the next. As a result, energy is carried through the water. The water itself is not moved.

There are two main kinds of waves. In a transverse wave, the motion of the particles in the medium is up and down or side to side. It is perpendicular to the direction of the wave's motion. In a longitudinal wave, the motion of the particles in the medium is back and forth, parallel to the direction of the wave's motion.

There are three main properties of waves: wavelength, frequency, and amplitude. Wavelength is the distance between a given point on one wave and the same point on the next wave. These points are usually the crest, or top, of the wave or the trough, or bottom, of the wave. If the crests of two waves are 1 inch apart, the wavelength is 1 inch.

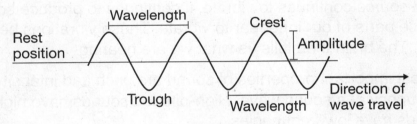

Parts of a Wave

Frequency is the number of waves that pass a point in one second. As wavelength gets shorter, frequency increases. If waves are closer together, more of them can pass a point in one second.

Amplitude is the distance from rest position to the crest or trough of a wave. The amplitude is related to the amount of energy carried by the wave. Higher energy equals greater amplitude.

Light we can see, X-rays, radio waves, and other forms of electromagnetic radiation also travel in waves. Electromagnetic waves are always transverse waves and do not need a medium to travel through. They can travel through empty space.

Sound Waves

Sound waves are created when things vibrate, or move back and forth quickly. Most sounds are a result of vibrations being carried through the air to your ears. Sound waves in air are longitudinal waves. The air molecules move back and forth in the direction the sound wave is traveling.

As something, such as a triangle musical instrument, vibrates forward and back, it pushes on nearby air molecules. The forward motion forces the air particles to move closer together. This is called compression. The back motion causes the air molecules to spread out. This is called rarefaction.

Sound waves travel through the air as a series of compressions and rarefactions. As long as the sound source continues to vibrate, it continues to produce sound waves. The sound waves cause parts of our inner ear to vibrate. These vibrations become signals that travel to the brain. The brain then tells us what we are hearing.

Two of the most important properties of sound are pitch and intensity. Pitch is related to the frequency of a sound wave. High-pitched sounds have high frequencies. Low-pitched sounds have low frequencies.

Sound intensity is related to a sound wave's amplitude. The higher the amplitude of the sound wave, the higher the intensity of the sound and the louder it is.

The Doppler Effect

Imagine a police car with its siren wailing is passing by you. When the car is approaching, the siren has a high pitch. After it passes, the pitch seems to get lower. The difference occurs because the source of the sound—the car—was in motion in relation to you. When it approached you, sound waves and their source were moving toward you. The sound waves got a boost in speed, so the wavelength was shorter, the pitch was higher, and the sound was louder.

When the car passed by, the opposite happened. The wavelength got longer, and the pitch was lower. But the sound's pitch only *seemed* to change. This apparent change in the frequency of a wave due to the motion of the source is the Doppler Effect.

Name _____   Date _____

How Do Waves Transfer Energy?

Write answers to the questions on the lines below.

1. What direction do the particles of the medium move in a transverse wave?

_____

_____

2. What direction do the particles of the medium move in a longitudinal wave?

_____

A   **B**   **C**   **D**

3. Why does wave A have a higher frequency than wave B?

_____

4. Why does wave D carry more energy than wave C?

_____

5. When are sound waves created?

_____

6. How is sound intensity related to the amplitude of a sound wave?

_____

7. What is the apparent change in the frequency of a wave caused by the motion of the source?

_____

8. Main Idea Give two examples of how waves transmit energy.

_____

_____

9. Vocabulary Compare a longitudinal wave and a transverse wave. Give one example of each kind of wave.

_____

_____

10. Reading Skill: Sequence Describe why a sound seems to increase in pitch when its source moves toward a listener.

_____

_____

11. Critical Thinking: Apply A car is traveling quickly past a non-moving police car. The police siren is blaring loudly. Does the Doppler effect apply? Explain.

_____

_____

12. Inquiry Skill: Record Data Make a chart to record these data for wind speed, amplitude, and wavelength: a 20-km/h wind causes ocean waves 0.3 m high and 10 m long, a 30-km/h wind causes waves 0.8 m high and 22 m long, and a 40-km/h wind causes waves 1.6 m high and 38 m long.

13. Test Prep Which is an example of waves that can travel through empty space?

   A sound waves   **C** longitudinal waves

   B light waves   **D** seismic waves

What Is the Electromagnetic Spectrum?

Light

Light is a form of electromagnetic radiation, or electromagnetic waves. An electromagnetic wave is made up of wave-shaped electric and magnetic fields. Light you can see, or visible light, makes up one part of a much larger band of radiation called the electromagnetic spectrum, or EM spectrum. The EM spectrum also includes gamma rays, X-rays, infrared radiation, microwaves, and radio waves.

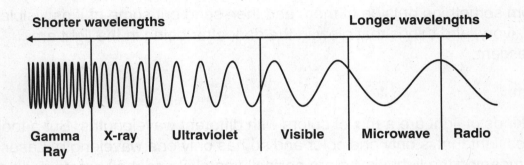

Shorter wavelengths ← → Longer wavelengths

Gamma Ray | X-ray | Ultraviolet | Visible | Microwave | Radio

Different parts of the EM spectrum have different wavelengths and frequencies. The higher a wave's frequency, the more energy it carries. Radio waves have the least energy, and gamma rays have the most.

All EM waves share some characteristics. They all can move through empty space. And they all move very, very fast. When electromagnetic waves enter matter, they slow down. Their speed depends on the kind of material they move through. When the wave slows down, its wavelength becomes shorter, but its frequency stays the same.

All electromagnetic waves also act both as waves and particles. Light particles are called photons, which are like tiny packets of energy.

Light can be made when photons interact with matter. When an electron in an atom absorbs a photon, the electron gains energy. When the electron returns to its normal state, it lets go of a proton and loses energy. That energy is in the form of light.

Making Light

Most things you see do not give off their own light. They reflect, or send back, light that hits them. You see them only because they reflect light back into your eyes. Over time, people have found ways to make light. Electric light bulbs are one way to make light. In a light bulb, an electric current flows through a wire called a filament, and the filament gives off light. This is called an incandescent light source. It gives off light made by heat.

There are other ways to make light. When an electric current is sent through certain gases, electrons in the gas atoms are excited. When the electrons return to an unexcited state, they send out light. These kinds of lights are called gas-discharge lights.

The most common gas-discharge lights are fluorescent lights. A fluorescent light is made of a glass tube with mercury vapor and a gas. The inside of the tube is coated with substances called phosphors. When an electric current excites the mercury vapor, the vapor sends out ultraviolet light. The ultraviolet photons hit the phosphors and excite their atoms. The atoms of the phosphors then send out that energy as visible light.

Some substances in nature make light through phosphorescence. They absorb energy from something outside of them and then send out some of it as visible light. Eggshells, ivory, and things that glow in the dark after being in the light are phosphorescent.

Laser Light

Most kinds of light are a mix of colors with different wavelengths. But a tool called a laser makes light that is only one color and so has only one wavelength. Laser light is also coherent, meaning the light waves are perfectly parallel and their crests and troughs line up. Coherent light is useful because it stays strong over a long stretch of space. It can also move great amounts of energy.

Laser stands for *Light Amplification by Stimulated Emission of Radiation*. Some lasers make powerful beams of light that can cut through steel. Others make light that is no more powerful than a flashlight beam.

Some lasers are used to check out our groceries and to read and write CDs and DVDs. Doctors and dentists use lasers for surgeries and repairs. Laser lights are used for light shows at theme parks, special effects in movies, and stage effects for concerts.

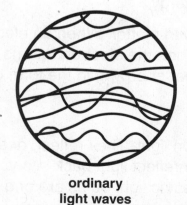

**ordinary
light waves**

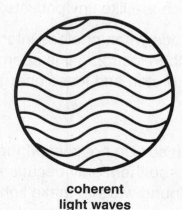

**coherent
light waves**

What Is the Electromagnetic Spectrum?

Fill in the blanks.

1. Light is a form of _____.

2. The higher a wave's frequency on the electromagnetic spectrum, the
   _____ energy it carries.

3. Light particles in electromagnetic waves are called _____.

Write answers to the questions on the lines below.

4. In addition to infrared radiation, visible light, and gamma rays, what other waves
   does the electromagnetic spectrum include?

   _____

5. When can light be produced?

   _____

6. What type of light source is a light bulb with a filament?

   _____

7. What substances absorb energy from an outside source and then emit some of it as
   visible light even after the source is removed?

   _____

8. Name two useful properties of coherent light.

   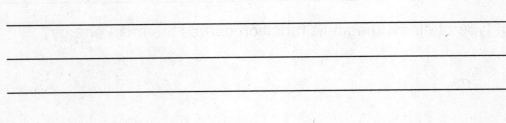 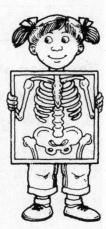

   _____

   _____

9. Main Idea Describe the electromagnetic spectrum.

_____

_____

10. Vocabulary Write a paragraph that explains the differences between incandescent, fluorescent, and laser light.

_____

_____

_____

11. Reading Skill: Main Idea and Details Explain how atoms can be made to emit light.

_____

_____

12. Critical Thinking: Infer Why does coherent light need to be all of one color?

_____

_____

13. Inquiry Skill: Predict Scientists continue to study electomagnetic radiation from space. Do you think this radiation may provide evidence of intelligent life on other planets? Explain your predictions.

_____

_____

_____

14. Test Prep Which type of electromagnetic radiation carries the most energy?

   A radio waves

   B visible light

   C X-rays

   D gamma rays

What Are Static and Current Electricity?

Electric Charges

Remember that all matter is made of atoms. Atoms are the basic building blocks of matter. They are very tiny. Yet atoms are made of even smaller particles. Two of these are protons and electrons. They carry electric charges. Protons carry positive charges, and electrons carry negative charges.

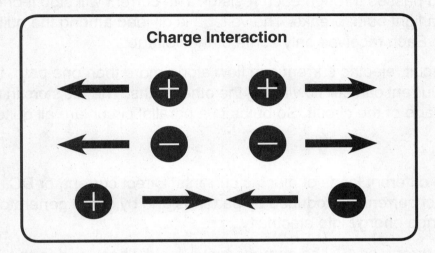

Charge Interaction

Look at the chart. A positive and a negative charge attract, or move toward, each other. Two positive charges repel, or move away, from each other. Two negative charges also repel each other. They attract or repel without touching. Charged particles and the forces among them are the source of electricity. Electricity is the movement or interaction of electric charges.

The word *static* means "at rest." Static electricity is a buildup of electric charges. The charges in static electricity are not moving.

To see static electricity at work, rub a balloon against a carpet. Then put the balloon next to a wall. The balloon will stick to the wall. This happens because the rubbing knocks electrons from the carpet to the balloon. The balloon now has a negative charge. It will attract the positive charges on the wall.

The force between two charged things is called electrostatic force. This force is greater when the charges of the object are greater and when many charges are close together.

Current electricity happens when charges are moving. Current electricity is the continuous net flow of electric charges from one place to another. The electric charges in current electricity are usually electrons, which move through a circuit, or closed loop. A switch turns the circuit on and off. A power source, such as a battery, sends electricity moving through the wires. Resistors change electrical energy to light or heat.

Volts and Amperes

Batteries supply voltage, the electric potential energy per unit charge. The greater a battery's voltage, the greater the electric current it can supply to the circuit. Voltage is measured in units called volts. The unit of measure for electric current is the ampere.

Types of Circuits

Electric circuits can be put together in different ways. In a series circuit, current flows along one path and passes through each resistor. The current will stop if one of the resistors, such as a light bulb, breaks. The voltage is divided among the bulbs, so they are not very bright. Each receives only some of the voltage.

In a parallel circuit, electric current can flow along more than one path. If a resistor in the circuit breaks, current can still flow along the other paths. The resistors in each pathway receive the full voltage of the circuit. So bulbs in a parallel circuit are all quite bright.

DC and AC

There are also different kinds of electric currents. Direct current, or DC, flows in one direction only. Direct current is produced by batteries and by some generators, which are machines that change energy into electricity.

In alternating current, or AC, the charges move rapidly back and forth through the circuit. Electricity delivered to homes is alternating current. Transformers are machines that are used to increase or decrease voltage.

Electric Circuits in the Home

How does current enter a home? Power plants send high voltage electricity through power lines. Transformers near homes decrease the voltage to a safe level. The low-voltage current travels to a circuit box inside a house. This box controls the flow of electricity to different circuits.

Wall switches and electric outlets are used in a house to control the flow of electricity. When a switch is turned on, electric current flows to a device. In most homes, the circuit box contains switches called circuit breakers, which open a circuit when too much current is flowing through it. This stops current from flowing and making circuits too hot.

Conductors and Insulators

A conductor is any material that allows electric charges to pass through it easily. Water and most metals are good conductors. A material that does not conduct electricity well is called an insulator. Wood, rubber, and plastic are insulators. The power cords of lamps are made of copper wire conductors wrapped in plastic or rubber insulation. This keeps the electricity flowing safely inside the wire.

What Are Static and Current Electricity?

Write answers to the questions on the lines below.

1. What does the word *static* mean?

_____

_____

2. What is the unit of measure for electric current?

_____

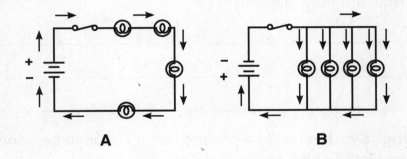

A　　　　　　　　　　**B**

3. Which circuit above would still have current flowing even if one of the resistors breaks?

_____

4. Why would light bulbs in circuit A be dimmer than bulbs in circuit B?

_____

_____

5. How do circuit breakers prevent circuits from overheating?

_____

_____

6. What devices reduce high-voltage current to safer, low-voltage current before it is used?

_____

© Houghton Mifflin Harcourt Publishing Company

7. Main Idea What is the difference between static electricity and current electricity?

_____

_____

8. Vocabulary Write a short paragraph about electrical current using the terms *conductor* and *insulator*.

_____

_____

9. Reading Skill: Compare and Contrast How are direct current and alternating current alike? How are they different?

_____

_____

_____

10. Critical Thinking: Synthesize Is it possible for a circuit to be connected both in series and in parallel? Explain.

_____

_____

11. Inquiry Skill: Predict A hair dryer that is plugged into an electric outlet is lying in a puddle of water. What would happen if you tried to pick up the dryer? Explain your answer.

_____

_____

12. Test Prep Which statement describes the electrostatic force between two charged objects?

A It is greater when two objects are farther apart.

B It is greater if two objects have the same charge.

C It is greater when the charges of the objects are greater.

D It is zero if the charges of the objects repel one another.

What Are Speed, Velocity, and Acceleration?

Distance and Speed

Motion is an object's change in position. You have to compare objects to other objects around them to describe motion and position. To describe the motion of a jogger, you would compare where he is to where something around him is. You could compare his position to the position of a tree.

Motion can be described as a measure of the distance an object moves in a certain length of time. Speed is a measure of how fast position changes. Speed compares the change in distance to the change in the time that has passed.

To measure speed, you use units of length and time. These are measures such as kilometers per hour (km/h) or miles per hour (mi/h). The speed of a moving object may change. A jogger's speed changes during his run. He runs faster on a level path than he does when he runs uphill. He runs fastest downhill. When he stops, time continues to pass, but he is not moving. His speed is zero.

Average speed is the total distance traveled divided by the total time it takes to go that distance. You can use a formula to figure average speed. The formula is:

$$\text{speed} = \frac{\text{distance}}{\text{time}}$$

Velocity and Acceleration

The term *velocity* describes the speed and direction of a moving object. An object's velocity can be constant or changing. An object might move without changing its speed or its direction. That object's velocity is constant. Velocity changes when an object changes speed, or direction, or both.

Acceleration happens when speed, or direction, or both change. Acceleration describes the rate at which velocity changes, but it can also be a change in direction. Speeding up or slowing down is acceleration, but so is turning left or right.

A small acceleration tells you that the velocity is changing slowly. A large acceleration tells you that the velocity is changing quickly.

Suppose the velocity of a car increases from 50 km/h to 80 km/h in 5 seconds. What is the average acceleration of the car?

First, find the change in velocity. The change in velocity is the difference between the ending velocity (v_2) and the beginning velocity (v_1). Then divide this difference by the time (t) that has passed. Use this formula to find average acceleration (a):

$$a = \frac{v_2 - v_1}{t}$$

In the example of the car, you can find that average acceleration of the car is 6 km/h per second. The car's velocity increases by 6 km/h each second.

$$a = \frac{80 \text{ km/h} - 50 \text{ km/h}}{5s} = 6 \text{ km/(h} \cdot \text{s)}$$

Frame of Reference

If you are sitting still in your classroom, you probably don't think you are moving. Compared to the room, you are in the same position. But Earth spins on its axis and also orbits the Sun. Astronauts might say that you are moving very quickly!

All motion is relative, meaning it is measured compared to some object. Scientists call this a frame of reference. A frame of reference is an object to which you choose to compare the motion of other objects.

Passengers inside a train are not moving relative to the train. The frame of reference of a person standing outside the train is different. To that person, the passengers are moving at the same velocity as the train—both are moving very quickly.

What Are Speed, Velocity, and Acceleration?

Write answers to the questions on the lines below.

1. What does speed compare?

   _____

2. How can two people start from the same point, travel at the same speed, and end up 100 kilometers apart?

   _____

3. What does velocity describe?

   _____

4. When does acceleration occur?

   _____

5. What is a frame of reference?

   _____

The formula below shows how to find the average acceleration of an object.

$$a = \frac{60 \text{ km/h} - 40 \text{ km/h}}{5s} = 4 \text{ km/(h} \cdot \text{s)}$$

6. What part of the formula represents the change in velocity?

   _____

7. What part of the formula represents the time that has passed?

   _____

8. Main Idea How is speed measured? Include example of units of speed.

_____

_____

9. Vocabulary Explain how the terms *speed*, *velocity*, and *acceleration* are related to each other.

_____

_____

_____

10. Reading Skill: Problem-Solution If a sprinter runs a distance of 100 m in 10 s, what is the sprinter's average speed?

_____

11. Critical Thinking: Analyze You are running east at a speed of 15 km/h. A car passes you traveling east at a speed of 50 km/h. You stop to wait for a bus and another car traveling east at a speed of 50 km/h passes you. How does your changing frame of reference affect how fast you observe each car as traveling?

_____

_____

12. Inquiry Skill: Predict How will punching a hole in a parachute affect the rate at which it falls?

_____

13. Test Prep Which describes velocity?

   A 10 km per second

   B 20 mi per hour

   C 3 m per second, due east

   D 15 cm along a ruler

What Are Newton's Laws?

Newton's First Law

It is hard to move a heavy object or to stop a fast-moving object. Objects that are at rest or moving tend to resist any change in motion. This is called inertia. All objects have inertia.

English scientist Sir Isaac Newton wrote three laws to describe forces and motion. Newton's first law describes inertia. Objects that are at rest or moving tend to resist any change in motion: an object at rest stays at rest, and an object in motion stays in motion. The greater the mass of the object, the greater its inertia and the greater the force needed to change its motion.

A force is needed to overcome an object's inertia. A force has magnitude, or size, and direction. The magnitude of a force is measured using a unit called the newton.

Look at the pictures of the objects on a scale. You can see that forces do not always cause a change in motion. Balanced forces are equal and do not cause a change in motion. Many different forces may act on an object. The motion of the object will change only if unbalanced forces act on it.

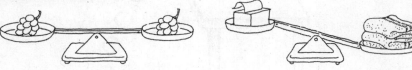

Friction

Friction is the force that opposes the motion of one surface against another. Friction occurs when there is motion between touching surfaces. Friction also acts on objects moving through water or air.

The amount of friction depends on the materials that are touching. A rubber puck may slide far across concrete. It will slide even farther across ice. A value called the coefficient of friction shows the amount of friction between surfaces. The higher the coefficient, the greater is the friction.

Friction always creates heat. Rub your hands together very quickly. Friction changes the energy of your moving hands into thermal energy, which warms up your hands.

Newton's Second Law

Newton's second law describes how force (F), mass (m), and acceleration (a) relate to each other. This relationship is written:

$$F = m \cdot a$$

Newton's second law shows that the greater the force, the greater the acceleration for a given mass. It also shows that the greater the mass, the smaller the acceleration for a given force.

Newton's Third Law

Newton's third law says that for every action force, there is an equal and opposite reaction force. Newton's third law means that forces come in pairs. Action and reaction forces act on different objects. If you are on roller skates, to change your motion you can push against a wall, which pushes back on you with an equal and opposite force. The harder you push, the greater your acceleration.

Gravitation

The force that causes objects to fall back to Earth is called gravitation. Gravitation is a force that attracts objects with mass toward each other without touching them. The gravitational attraction by Earth on object at or near its surface is usually called gravity.

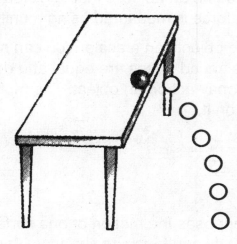

Newton found that the strength of the gravitational force between two objects depends on two things: mass and distance. The greater the masses of the objects, the stronger the gravitational force is between them. The smaller the distance between the two objects, the stronger the gravitational force. The greater the distance, the weaker the force.

Mass and Weight

Mass and weight are different. Mass is the amount of matter in an object. The amount of matter in an object is the same no matter if the object is on Earth, the Moon, or in outer space.

Weight is a force. It is the pull of gravity on a mass. The weight of an object is equal to the mass of the object multiplied by the acceleration caused by gravity. Weight depends on where the object is located. For example, the gravitation acceleration on the Moon is less than that of Earth. So a person who weighs 590 newtons on Earth weighs only 96 newtons on the Moon.

What Are Newton's Laws?

Fill in the blanks.

1. Newton's first law describes the tendency called _____.

2. Newton's first law of motion states that without the action of a(n)

   _____, an object at rest stays at rest and an object in motion stays in motion.

3. The magnitude of a force is measured using a unit called the

   _____.

4. _____ is a force that opposes the motion of one surface against another.

5. The relationship described in Newton's second law can be written as

   _____.

6. Newton's third law means that all forces come in _____.

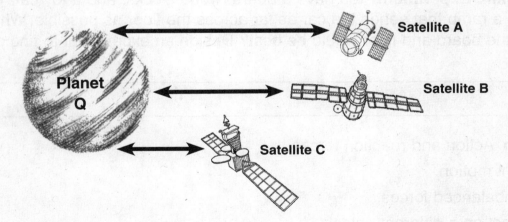

7. In the diagram above, Satellite _____ will have the least gravitational pull toward Planet Q.

8. In the diagram above, Satellite _____ will have the greatest gravitational pull toward Planet Q.

9. Main Idea Explain how force, mass, and acceleration are related.

_____

_____

10. Vocabulary Use the terms *inertia* and *force* to describe Newton's first law of motion.

_____

_____

11. Reading Skill: Main Idea How do distance and mass affect the force of gravity?

_____

_____

_____

12. Critical Thinking: Analyze Many highways with steep hills have ramps for trucks that are moving too quickly. Why would trucks have a harder time than cars slowing down on steep hills?

_____

_____

13. Inquiry Skill: Experiment You have a board, wood blocks, and a toy car. Your goal is to build a ramp that sends the car as far across the floor as possible. What angle between the board and floor would be best? Design an experiment to find out.

_____

_____

14. Test Prep Action and reaction forces

  A prevent motion.

  B are unbalanced forces.

  C each act on a different object.

  D each act in the same direction.

Answer Key

How Do Scientists Classify Organisms?

1. "Dichotomous" means "divided into two parts," so the key gives two characteristics to choose between. Each choice leads to another pair of characteristics and narrows the possibility of what the organism could be.
2. Bacteria in your stomach help you digest food.
3. bacteria
4. They do not make their own food. They can move.
5. protist   6. archaebacteria
7. to give an organism a name recognized by scientists all over the world, to group organisms by characteristics
8. a system that organizes living things into groups
9. protist kingdom
10. Sample answer: Some organisms lacked characteristics associated with either kingdom.
11. Most protists can move, but fungi cannot. Fungi get nutrients by breaking down organic matter, and protists create their own food.
12. C

How Are Plants Classified?

1. seed sprouts and a new plant grows
2. gets pollinated
3. the petals fall off
4. grows and becomes the fruit
5. matures and protects the seeds inside
6. true   7. false   8. true
9. how the plants transport water; how plants reproduce
10. Vascular plants have tube-like tissues that transport water and nutrients.
11. Angiosperms produce flowers, fruit, and seeds. Gymnosperms produce seeds, but no flowers or fruits.
12. No, plants produce fruits to protect and nourish seeds.
13. Yes, vascular plants would have visible vascular tissues.
14. D

How Are Animals Classified?

1. c   2. e   3. b
4. d   5. a   6. bird
7. reptile   8. mammal
9. amphibian
10. They have complex organs and nervous systems, they have hair, and they feed milk to their young, which are born live.
11. Animals have different shapes, skin coverings, body structures, and body temperatures.
12. Invertebrates are animals that lack a backbone. Vertebrates are animals that have a backbone.
13. sponges: lack true body symmetry, shapeless bodies; cnidarians: radial symmetry, mouths; echinoderms: radial symmetry, catch prey with suckers; worms: bilateral symmetry, clearly defined heads; mollusks: bilateral symmetry, soft bodies, sometimes hard shell; arthropods: bilateral symmetry, movable joints
14. Birds are the only animals with feathers, so it would have to be a bird. Not all birds can fly.
15. Charts should show levels of vertebrate classification: coldblooded: fish, amphibians, reptiles; warmblooded: birds, mammals
16. C

What Do Cells Do?

1. cell   2. nucleus
3. diffusion   4. Osmosis
5. low, high   6. glucose
7. cell division   8. chloroplasts
9. Mitochondria
10. Cells need food, water, and a way to eliminate wastes.
11. Sample answer: A chloroplast is an organelle in plant cells that makes food for the plant.
12. No, it could not survive because the mitochondria provides energy to the cell.
13. cell membrane: lets material in and out and keeps cell together; nucleus: directs all cell activities; cytoplasm: surrounds nucleus and organelles
14. Diffusion spreads substances through a gas or liquid, so the substance, food coloring, is being spread through the liquid, water.
15. A

How Are Cells Specialized?

1. Glands   2. epithelial
3. organ   4. organ systems
5. Hormones   6. B   7. B
8. Cells with the ability to perform certain tasks are specialized cells.
9. Sample answer: Tissue is a group of cells with the same structure and function. Epithelial tissue protects surfaces.
10. Sample answer: The respiratory system brings oxygen into the body; the circulatory system carries it to cells.
11. No, different species might have different needs, so the organs will be different.

12. The nervous system sends information and signals to and from the brain.
13. D

How Do Oxygen and Carbon Dioxide Cycle?

1. photosynthesis
2. Energy from sunlight is used to change carbon dioxide and water into glucose and oxygen.
3. respiration
4. Oxygen and glucose are combined to produce carbon dioxide and water. Then stored energy is released.
5. burning fossil fuels and cutting down trees
6. Both plants and animals need oxygen for respiration, and plants need carbon dioxide for photosynthesis.
7. Sample answer: Photosynthesis is opposite to respiration.
8. Photosynthesis uses carbon dioxide and releases oxygen; respiration uses oxygen and releases carbon dioxide.
9. No, there is much less carbon dioxide than oxygen.
10. It will decrease because the algae will use the carbon dioxide for photosynthesis.
11. D

How Do Nitrogen and Water Cycle?

1. nitrogen fixation   2. decomposition
3. evaporation   4. condensation
5. precipitation   6. 1 percent
7. pollution
8. Both substances are necessary for life, so they need to be recycled.
9. Evaporation changes water from a liquid to a gas; transpiration is the evaporation of water from a plant's leaves.
10. nitrogen fixation; from lightning or the action of bacteria
11. It is scarce in some places, and an increasing number of people on Earth means more water will be used, making it more scarce.
12. Transpiration from leaves no longer adds water vapor to the air. This means less water will condense and fall as precipitation. These areas may get drier.
13. C

What Are Earth's Ecosystems?

1. animals, plants, and microorganisms
2. temperature, precipitation, wind, and soil
3. the average weather conditions in a place from year to year
4. a large group of similar ecosystems

5. The taiga is warmer and wetter than the tundra.
6. Temperate forests get enough rainfall to support trees, but grasslands are too dry to support trees.
7. oceanic zone   8. neritic zone
9. intertidal zone
10. Organisms that live in a desert must survive abiotic factors of high temperatures and lack of water.
11. Biodiversity is the variety of organisms in an area. Tropical rain forests have the greatest biodiversity because of the year-round warm temperatures and lots of rain.
12. Each zone has different characteristics. The species in each zone are adapted to those characteristics.
13. Animals adapted to cold climates might have trouble surviving because they would be too warm.
14. You could infer that it lives in the oceanic zone. That zone is very deep and dark, so the fish has adapted to this environment by making its own light.
15. C

What Role Do Species Play?

1. its relationship with the biotic and abiotic factors of the ecosystem
2. Their presence indicates an ecosystem is healthy because they cannot survive without healthy numbers of other plant and animal populations.
3. Raccoons will eat almost anything.
4. Producers   5. Carnivores
6. decomposers
7. They depend on other organisms for nutrients. Each species must remain healthy to keep the entire system healthy.
8. Both will eat animals; an omnivore will also eat plants.
9. producers: oak tree, cactus, grass; herbivores: deer, rabbit; carnivore: rattlesnake; omnivore: raccoon
10. hawk; because it is at the top of the food chain
11. Sample answer: I would measure the concentration of DDT in animals at or near the top of the food chain.
12. D

What Limits Population Growth?

1. hawk and owl hunting the same prey
2. wolves eating deer
3. Dutch elm disease
4. false   5. true   6. true
7. one stressed by overcrowding or lack of food and water
8. Sample: A limiting factor restricts the growth of a population. Predation is one important limiting factor.
9. habitat loss, disease, loss of food source, increased predators, invasive species

10. There are too many deer, and the ecosystem cannot support them. Decreasing the deer population to the carrying capacity will help balance the ecosystem.
11. The number of coyotes will increase because there are no natural predators in the neighborhood to control the population.
12. D

What Are the Three Classes of Rock?

1. A   2. B   3. C
4. heat and pressure
5. melting   6. cooling
7. uplifting   8. uplifting
9. They form as magma cools and minerals crystallize.
10. Sample answer: The rock cycle is a process during which one type of rock is changed into another type. For example, sedimentary rock becomes metamorphic rock.
11. Both are formed when magma cools beneath the Earth's surface. If it cools quickly, small crystals form. If it cools slowly, large crystals form.
12. The area where the rock originally formed was underwater. Either the region was pushed up, or the water receded to reveal the rock.
13. It is probably sedimentary rock.
14. C

What Are Tectonic Plates?

1. crust   2. lithosphere
3. mantle   4. outer core
5. inner core   6. true
7. false   8. false   9. true
10. Hot, soft rock in the mantle below the plates moves slowly in huge loops called convection cells, which move the plates.
11. Sample answer: The lithosphere is made up of Earth's crust and the top part of the mantle.
12. Rift valleys appear on the floor of the world's oceans where sea-floor spreading occurs. By studying sea-floor spreading, scientists learned much about how plate tectonics works.
13. Sea-floor spreading creates new ocean floor when two plates move apart.
14. Answers will vary but should support the ideas behind the process of sea-floor spreading.
15. B

What Changes Do Moving Plates Cause?

1. Himalaya Mountains
2. where two plates slide horizontally past each other
3. convergent   4. San Andreas Fault
5. divergent

6. where plates are moving apart
7. epicenter   8. magma
9. mountain chains, volcanoes, and earthquakes
10. Sample answer: The focus of an earthquake is where movement first occurs; the epicenter is above the focus.
11. Earthquakes occur when stress builds up between moving plates. Seismic waves collapse structures, hurting people
12. volcanic activity, earthquakes, movement at plate boundary; the island may widen as the plates continue to move
13. The focus and epicenter must be in the neighborhood because the shaking is worse at the epicenter. The seismic waves were also worse in the neighborhood because they are worse at the focus.
14. C

Why Are Fossil Fuels Limited?

1. natural gas, coal, and oil
2. the Sun
3. They cannot be replaced quickly or easily.
4. Turn off lights and appliances. Recycle materials. Change clothes to fit the weather. Seal windows and doors.
5. 4, 2, 3, 1
6. The remains of organisms are pressed together over time. They are found in swamps and in the ocean floor.
7. Sample answer: Fossil fuels are nonrenewable resources because they take millions of years to form. They cannot be replaced easily, so they should be used wisely.
8. making stricter laws and creating new energy sources
9. Fossil fuels provide excellent sources of energy to fulfill our energy needs. However, they are nonrenewable resources and burning them makes air and water pollution. Scientists are looking for new energy sources to reduce our dependence on fossil fuels.
10. Answers will vary but should illustrate the idea that coal is formed in layers as organisms die, decay, and get pressed together.
11. C

How Can Renewable Energy Be Used?

1. e   2. d   3. f
4. b   5. c   6. a
7. g
8. hydroelectric power
9. solar and wind power
10. biomass
11. Hydrogen fuel cells release energy with no harmful byproducts.

Electricity fuels cars using rechargeable batteries.

12. Hydroelectric energy is electric energy generated from moving water. Moving water turns turbines. The energy from the turbines is converted into electricity.
13. It is once-living matter with stored energy. It renews as organisms die and become waste.
14. Sample answer: Fossil fuels are limited, and nuclear energy is not. Burning fossil fuels creates pollution, but nuclear reactions create deadly waste.
15. Sample answer: a simple pinwheel
16. C

Why Does Weather Occur?

1. reflected
2. absorbs
3. surface
4. Cold air is denser than warm air, so it sinks.
5. a convection current
6. rain, snow, hail, sleet, or mist that falls to Earth's surface from clouds
7. from the area over which they form
8. the place where two air masses meet along a boundary
9. a body of air with similar temperature and water vapor throughout
10. Sample answer: Two air masses that meet along a front have different temperatures and pressures. These differences often cause precipitation.
11. Both are formed from water droplets. Cumulus clouds look puffy, and stratus clouds look layered.
12. You would expect rain or a thunderstorm.
13. 0, 100°C; 1,500, 95°C; 3,000, 90°C
14. A

How Can Storms Be Tracked?

1. Doppler
2. front
3. cumulonimbus
4. unstable
5. Lightning
6. blizzards
7. hurricane
8. Tornadoes
9. Warm, moist air rises above cooler air and forms cumulonimbus clouds.
10. Sample answer: A tornado can develop during a severe thunderstorm.
11. Hurricanes start as thunderstorms over warm, tropical oceans. The thunderstorms intensify and start rotating around the low-pressure zone, forming a hurricane.
12. Hurricanes cover a larger area and move slowly. Tornadoes can have higher wind speeds that cover a narrower path and do not last as long.
13. Hurricanes lose strength because they no longer have large amounts of water vapor to fuel cloud development.
14. B

How Does the Sun Affect Earth?

1. star
2. energy
3. rotates
4. revolution
5. Los Angeles
6. Northern
7. constellations
8. Earth revolves around the Sun at a tilt. This affects the hours of sunlight that areas receive throughout the year.
9. Earth's rotation is the spinning of Earth on its axis. Earth's revolution is the orbiting of Earth around the Sun.
10. The Sun keeps Earth in orbit; it powers photosynthesis; it lights Earth; it heats Earth.
11. In summer, you can see a constellation's position while your hemisphere faces the Sun. By winter, Earth has orbited halfway around the Sun. You then face away from the constellation.
12. It is spring (in the Northern Hemisphere).
13. B

How Do Eclipses Occur?

1. As the Moon orbits Earth, different portions of the lit part are visible from Earth.
2. the umbra and the penumbra
3. the corona
4. A planetary transit occurs when a planet passes between the Sun and Earth.
5. Venus and Mercury
6. A solar eclipse occurs when the Moon is between the Sun and Earth and the Moon's shadow falls on Earth. A lunar eclipse occurs when Earth is between the Sun and moon and Earth's shadow falls on the moon.
7. umbra: the darker, central region of Earth's shadow; penumbra: fainter region that surrounds the umbra
8. Sample answer: full moon, waning moon, last quarter, waning crescent
9. The Moon is between the Sun and Earth. Its illuminated side faces entirely away from Earth.
10. It lies outside Earth's orbit.
11. B

What Causes Tides?

1. tidal bulges
2. each day
3. spring tides
4. neap tides
5. tidal range
6. the shape of the land and the depth of the water
7. Tides are the daily changes in the ocean level. They are caused by the Moon's gravitational pull on oceans.
8. Sample answer: The tidal range is greater during spring tides than during neap tides.
9. The Sun and Moon are aligned, so they pull the ocean water more strongly.

10. The Moon's gravitational pull would be weaker, and Earth's tidal bulges would be smaller.
11. The difference is greater for spring tides because they result from the pull of both the Moon and the Sun.
12. A

What Are Building Blocks of Matter?

1. atom
2. ion
3. isotopes
4. radioactive
5. Periodic Table
6. atomic number
7. atomic number
8. chemical symbol
9. element name
10. Protons and neutrons are found in the nucleus. Electrons are found in the large area outside the nucleus.
11. Sample answer: A positive ion has fewer electrons than protons.
12. Rutherford devised the theory that an atom has a positive nucleus surrounded by negative electrons.
13. They all have similar properties.
14. calcium: protons = 20, neutrons = 20, electrons = 20; carbon-14: protons = 6, neutrons = 8, electrons = 6; lithium: protons = 3, neutrons = 3, electrons = 3
15. B

What Is Physical Change?

1. kinetic
2. thermal
3. pressure
4. expand
5. increases
6. melting point
7. vaporization
8. When the temperature increases, average speed increases.
9. Temperature is a measure of average kinetic energy of a substance. Thermal energy is the total kinetic energy of a substance.
10. The volume of a gas decreases.
11. The solid underwent a state change and became a liquid at 0°C.
12. It was warmer outside than inside. The increased temperature caused the volume of air particles inside the balloons to exceed the capacity of the space.
13. A

What Is Chemical Change?

1. One set of substances changes to form new substances.
2. Existing bonds are broken and new bonds are formed.
3. endothermic reaction
4. exothermic
5. absorb
6. light, heat, sound
7. Chemical changes involve breaking and forming of bonds. Energy is needed to do both.
8. An endothermic reaction absorbs energy, while an exothermic reaction releases energy.
9. The substances that form have different properties and

compositions than the substances that react.
10. exothermic; It releases energy in the form of light.
11. change in color; production of heat, light, or sound
12. B

What Are Types of Chemical Reactions?

1. chemical equation 2. arrow
3. mass   4. synthesis
5. decomposition
6. single replacement
7. double replacement
8. combustion
9. synthesis, decomposition, single-replacement, double-replacement, combustion
10. Balanced chemical equations show that the numbers and types of atoms are the same on both sides of the arrow.
11. The formation of sodium chloride from sodium and chlorine is a synthesis reaction.
12. It is a synthesis reaction because two substances react to form a single substance. It is a combustion reaction because a substance reacts with oxygen to form water.
13. The right side of the equation has more atoms. The balanced equation is: $Zn + 2HCl \longrightarrow ZnCl_2 + H_2$
14. C

What Is Conservation of Energy?

1. created or destroyed
2. kinetic   3. potential
4. nuclear   5. kinetic
6. Chemical   7. kinetic
8. Energy can't be created or destroyed, it can be transformed from one kind to another, and it can be potential or kinetic.
9. potential: stored energy; kinetic: energy of motion. A person holding a ball has potential energy, which becomes kinetic energy when he or she throws the ball.
10. Plants would not grow, which means people would have nothing to eat.
11. The blender loses energy from friction.
12. In fusion, small nuclei join together; fission involves splitting nuclei.
13. D

How Do Waves Transfer Energy?

1. perpendicular to the motion of the wave
2. parallel to the motion of the wave
3. Wave A has a shorter wavelength.
4. Wave D has a greater amplitude.
5. when objects vibrate
6. the higher the amplitude, the higher the intensity
7. the Doppler Effect
8. Waves transmit energy through water or air.
9. longitudinal: back and forth, example: sound wave; transverse: move up and down, example: electromagnetic wave
10. The movement gives the sound waves a boost in frequency and makes them sound louder and higher pitched.
11. Yes, the Doppler Effect applies because the sound is moving in relation to the listener.
12. wind speed—20 km/h, amplitude—0.3 m, wavelength—10 m; wind speed—30 km/h, amplitude—0.8 m, wavelength—22 m; wind speed—40 km/h, amplitude—1.6 m, wavelength—38 m
13. B

What Is the Electromagnetic Spectrum?

1. electromagnetic radiation
2. more   3. photons
4. radio waves, microwaves, and X-rays
5. Light can be produced when photons interact with matter.
6. an incandescent light source
7. phosphorescent substances
8. It can be concentrated over long distances, and it can transfer great amounts of energy.
9. It organizes radiation according to energy level.
10. Incandescent energy is created by glowing objects. Fluorescent light is created by vapor that produces photons that eventually change to light. Coherent light is a single color.
11. When energy is added to an atom, electrons gain energy. When they return to normal, they lose energy, which is emitted as light.
12. It if had waves with different wavelengths, the waves' crests and troughs would not line up.
13. Students' predictions will vary.
14. D

What Are Static and Current Electricity?

1. at rest   2. amperes
3. circuit B
4. Since the light bulbs are connected in series, there is a voltage drop across each bulb.
5. They open a circuit when too much current is flowing through it.
6. transformers
7. Static electricity is isolated electric charges at rest in objects; current electricity is continuous flow of charges.
8. Sample answer: Electric current passes easily through a conductor and is stopped by an insulator.
9. Electrons flow from one point to another in both. DC current flows in only one direction, but AC current flows back and forth through a circuit.
10. Yes. In parts of the circuit, resistors may be in a series, and in others, they may be parallel.
11. You would receive an electric shock. Water is a good conductor of electricity, so the water would pass the dryer's electricity on to you.
12. C

What Are Speed, Velocity, and Acceleration?

1. the change in distance to the amount of elapsed time
2. They went in different directions.
3. the speed and direction of a moving object
4. when speed, direction, or both change
5. an object to which you compare the motion of all other objects
6. 60 km/h – 40 km/h
7. 5s
8. Speed is measured by dividing distance by time. Units of speed include km/h and mi/h.
9. All three describe an object's motion.
10. 10 m/s
11. The second car will seem faster than the first car.
12. It will fall faster.
13. C

What Are Newton's Laws?

1. inertia   2. force
3. newton   4. Friction
5. $F = m \cdot a$ 6. pairs
7. A   8. C
9. The mass of an object times acceleration equals force.
10. Newton's first law states that force can be used to overcome inertia.
11. The force of gravity between two objects increases as their mass increases and decreases as the distance between them increases.
12. A large mass has more inertia than a small mass.
13. Designs should include systematically changing the slope angle while holding other factors constant.
14. C